As someone who has often p███████████████████ ose-
tinted spectacles in order to le██ D1454250 ████ .any
biblical characters, Jeannie's la█████████████████ ome
in handy! Her vivid re-imaginings of characters both well-known
and barely known is imaginative as it is impressive; and her application of their reimagined stories to our contemporary experiences, especially in the struggle, is both inspiring and relevant.

Revd Phil Barnard, regional team leader, London Baptists

Heroes or Villains is a refreshingly honest reflection upon some
well-known and not so well-known Bible characters. Jeannie's
ingenious exploration into their lives reveals fresh and provoca-
tive insights, with outstanding application for individual or group
study, underpinned by years of counselling experience, outstanding theological reflection and an enviable talent in creative writing.

Revd Chris Brockway, minister, Christchurch Baptist Church

In this her third book, Jeannie Kendall has once again contempo-
rised the biblical narrative in an accessible and imaginative way.
Her clarification of background to the narrative, where helpful, is
second to none. Jeannie has the ability to illuminate qualities and
emotions that may be experienced by each one of us, adding, as
ever, to the richness of our understanding of ourselves and others.

Dr Rachel E. Johnson, retired academic librarian,
volunteer, Hereford Cathedral

A refreshing opportunity to engage with important themes
viewed in the context of biblical characters. The application
questions provide further challenge to live out our faith in a
mature and integrated way.

Mrs Rosanne Tyas, music therapist, worship leader, wife,
mother and grandmother

Heroes or Villains is a gift. Throughout its pages we are offered wisdom, insight and grace. Jeannie's creativity and thoughtfulness in writing enables us to explore our reality and our hope in a way that is both accessible and profound. I'm glad I read it. I'm sure you will be too . . .

Revd David R. Mayne, lead pastor,
Shoeburyness and Thorpe Bay Baptist Church

Combining a gift for storytelling and an acute awareness of the psychological dynamics that affect women and men, Jeannie Kendall has explored the characters of people in the Scriptures – heroes as well as villains – in a way that brings them alive for a twenty-first-century audience. The combination of faithfulness to the witness of the Bible and an understanding of the inner workings of the psyche give this book its power to resource the spirit and engage the reader in their everyday discipleship. It certainly reveals the wisdom of Solomon (Chapter 8), the generosity of the widow (Chapter 14) and the honesty of Thomas (Chapter 18) in every chapter, each of which might serve as a small group Bible study, or an extended daily Scripture reading, meditation and prayerful response.

Revd Dr Paul Goodliff, former general secretary,
Churches Together in England

This is a wonderful book which is accessible with short chapters, sensitively written, but also deeply challenging. We are enabled to look at twenty different themes such as loyalty, vulnerability, insecurity, courage, and betrayal through the stories of very human and flawed biblical characters, some better known than others. But be warned, some of your assumption of who is a hero and who is villain may get challenged!

Jeannie encourages us to reflect on their stories and then our own character and life. The questions at the end of each chapter are particularly helpful, offering both challenge and encouragement. This is suitable for individuals and groups.

Revd Julie Aylward, prison chaplain

I love the way Jeannie in this book reveals the deep research and creativity that she has instilled into *Heroes or Villains*, characters I thought I knew about, but see them now in a new and refreshing way. As you read through, you also see aspects of your own life being highlighted, good and bad, and are made aware where change is required and developed further. Thank you, Jeannie, for yet another masterpiece.

Dave Lock, manager of Manna Christian Centre,
Streatham, London

As a former member of the Parole Board for England and Wales, I had to look at what an offender had done, but more importantly what was driving their behaviour, their own insights and whether they had changed. Jeannie's book reminds me very much of what I used to do, because she takes some twenty characters from the Bible and looks at what they did (good or bad), the cultural context of their time and what may have been behind their actions. Inevitably, some of her narrative is speculative (after all, the Bible is concise in its accounts) but it makes fascinating reading and sometimes it is eye-opening. I enjoyed reading this book, and at times I found myself saying 'But for the Grace of God . . .' just as I did when I was at the Parole Board. Full of insight, it challenges the concept that everyone is either good or bad and shows that there are many areas in life that are grey.

Cedric Pierce, formerly independent member
of the Parole Board for England and Wales

Sometimes we can find it hard to relate to biblical characters. We either see them as far better than we are, 'heroes'; or far worse than we are, 'villains'. The truth is that there is light and dark in all of us and we are far more complex than we often realise, and because of that we can find points of connection in almost all we come across.

That's certainly true in this book. Jeannie not only creatively gives voice to a wonderful range of biblical characters, but in doing so helps us to see the light and dark in our own lives, as well as the shades in-between.

With helpful reflection questions at the end of each chapter, this is a book that not only helps us explore Scripture, but ourselves too, all under the banner of God's lavish love.

Andy Percey, pastor and author

Heroes or Villains?

Exploring the qualities we share with Bible characters

Jeannie Kendall

Authentic

First published 2023 by Authentic Media Limited,
PO Box 6326, Bletchley, Milton Keynes, MK1 9GG.
authenticmedia.co.uk

British Library Cataloguing in Publication Data
A catalogue record for this book is available from the British Library.
ISBN: 978-1-78893-298-1
978-1-78893-299-8 (e-book)

Cover design by Vivian Hansen (Two Rivers Creative)
Printed and bound by CPI Group (UK) Ltd, Croydon, CR0 4YY

Dedication

To all those teachers over the years who have brought alive the Scriptures in preaching and practice, in particular Mike Wood, who I had the joy of working with at Streatham Baptist Church (known as 'Lewin'), and his wife, Lesley, who exemplified such quiet service.

To the church communities of Camborne Parish Church, Streatham Baptist Church, Carshalton Beeches Baptist Church, Woodmansterne Baptist Church and Christchurch Baptist Church, all of whom have been a part of my spiritual journey through the years.

To my precious family, who keep me grounded, especially with the searching questions of my wonderful grandchildren.

And above all to God, my companion in every season.

Contents

Contents

Foreword

In 1979, the Boomtown Rats released a song called, 'I Don't Like Mondays'. While I am aware of the background to this song, I *do* like Mondays. Because every Monday a new poem from Jeannie Kendall appears on Facebook which makes for an excellent start to the week. Jeannie likes words – and uses them well – as we can see in her poems and two previous books: *Finding Our Voice*, and *Held in Your Bottle*. *Heroes or Villains* is no exception.

On seeing the title, it would be only reasonable to assume it concerns heroes and villains. But Jeannie is far too wise a traveller to have taken that polarised path, and recognises that our heroes are never altogether good nor our villains altogether bad. Jezebel, as she points out, 'has come to epitomise the personification of an evil woman' but, and here we go, 'Perhaps, however, there is rather more to her.' This is what makes the book so captivating and enjoyable. As Jeannie writes, 'We each hold within us the potential for great good and disastrous moral failure.' As human beings we are a complex mixture.

I met Jeannie in 1986. In the intervening years I have known her as counsellor, pastor, lecturer and pastor to pastors, as author and as friend. Those who have read her previous books will know that she writes with a wealth of insight into the

Scriptures, theology, spirituality and psychology, combined with a wide experience of life. And while she is easy to read, don't be fooled. This stuff has depth. Choosing twenty biblical characters, Jeannie explores each within the framework of an imaginative first-person narrative, followed by a passage of scripture, an exploration of the key theme, and then some questions for reflection to earth this in the experience of the reader. In her exploration of the key theme, Jeannie shares insights from her rich experience, expanding our understanding of themes such as protest, power and prejudice.

This is a book that will nourish those who are new to faith and those who have become more established. It is a book that engages with the reality of who we are and also the reality of the God who is with us, or as Jeannie puts it, 'the lavish way in which God loves us deeply as we are, mixed and muddled, villainous and heroic.' A theme which has become significant for me is being attentive to rhythms of grace. What shines out from this book is Jeannie's embodiment of this attentiveness to a grace-filled life. May this be your experience as you read *Heroes or Villains*.

Revd Geoff Colmer, former regional team leader for Central Baptist Association and past president of the Baptist Union

Introduction

Some time ago I was discussing The Avengers[1] with my (then) 6-year-old grandson. As I am by no means an expert, I asked him whether a character he had just named was 'a goodie or a baddie'. As soon as I spoke the words, it started a train of thought of which this book is the result.

We love to divide the world in that way, don't we? Dramas are at the most satisfying when the 'goodies' win after a period of intense struggle. We are both frustrated and fascinated when, tainted by reality, the outcome is not that simple.

Some years ago, a film trilogy was released based on the novel *The Lord of the Rings*, by J.R.R. Tolkien.[2] The hero, Frodo, is tasked with destroying a ring which will bring untold power to Sauron, the villain, something which must be done by dropping it into a lake of fire. I know the story well, yet watching the film found myself shouting inwardly (thankfully not outwardly!) towards the end, 'Drop the ring! Just drop the ring!' In that moment, Frodo is himself overcome and cannot destroy it. Hero he may be, perfect he is not, and ironically the ring is eventually, accidentally, destroyed by Gollum, himself a most complex character who, in the film, is clearly shown battling the twin sides of his nature. St Paul himself of course knew a similar struggle: 'For I do not do the good I want to do, but the evil I do not want to do – this I keep on doing.'[3]

Yet still we want to divide the world more clearly, and see ourselves and others in those simple terms. The psychoanalyst Melanie Klein[4] describes how from a pre-verbal stage we mentally 'split' people and experiences into 'good' and 'bad' as a way to try to make sense of the world. As we grow, we are able to hold a more nuanced view, but it remains a struggle at times to do so.

When I first proposed this book to Authentic, I had intended to only look at biblical villains, to show that those qualities which marked them out in that way were present, at least potentially, in us too. The suggestion came back to include 'heroes' as well, and I immediately thought of those who are seen as heroes of faith and yet whose behaviour was at times reprehensible, such as David, described as a man after God's own heart[5] yet failing so catastrophically in his personal life. However, this dichotomy is the whole premise of this book. Like the characters we find in the Bible, we each hold within us the potential for great good and disastrous moral failure. We will inevitably not live up to our own expectation of ourselves at times – but the overall pattern of our choices really matters in the building, over time, of our character. The specific quality I will consider in relation to each character does not define them – as with us, it is one aspect of the complex person they were.

The book can be read individually or used as a basis for small group study and discussion, and each chapter has the same format. The sections are an imaginative retelling of part of their Bible story from the perspective of the character featured in the chapter, the Bible text (to enable the book to be given to someone who might not have a Bible, and for ease of use), an exploration of one aspect of that particular person, and some questions for reflection. I hope whatever the context in which you read it, it will help you to recognise more the complexity of your own character as much as those of the biblical individuals, and through that to experience for the first time, or again, the lavish way in which God loves us deeply as we are, mixed and muddled, villainous and heroic.

Adam and Eve: Dissatisfaction

*The woman said to the snake, 'We may eat fruit
from the trees in the garden, but God did say,
"You must not eat fruit from the tree that is
in the middle of the garden, and you must not
touch it, or you will die."'*

Gen. 3:2–3

The voice of Adam

It was all so beautiful. When I first woke from what seemed an eternal slumber, blinking at the light as I opened my eyes, my senses were overwhelmed by a riot of colour, fragrance, sound. As I stood uncertainly to my feet, the earth was soft and welcoming, as if my skin and the gentle tendrils of growth beneath were one. Around me birds, as I would later name them, fluttered: each brought in front of me by my constant Companion and Friend. They watched me, curiously but without a hint of wariness. Butterflies kissed the flowers for the briefest of moments, at times resting on my arm as I watched. Trees reached for the sky, standing like silent benign sentinels, as if guarding the purity of the land. As time passed, in the day I would watch the sun dancing on their leaves, and at night I would marvel at the moon, glimpsing it through their branches.

Life was so simple. Water in a coconut I had broken on a rock. Fruits and berries, nuts and plants to eat. Bathing in the river, drying in the sunshine. But the true beauty, the crowning glory, came with the woman. She was sublime. Finally, I felt complete. Her soft flesh, her body moulding itself to mine. Our eyes meeting in a silent language of our own. We laughed, we danced, we ran through the garden with delight as we explored. It was perfect.

Why, I wonder now, did I listen to that inner voice? There was only one limit for us, one tree in all that vast array, that we were not to eat. Just one. At first, I did not find it difficult. I had so much – we had so much. Why would we want that one tree when we had the whole garden?

And yet day by day the inner voice got stronger, hissing insistently in my ear. 'Why can't you eat that one? Is it so delicious your Creator wants to keep it for themself? Why should you not have it too? After all, you are rulers here, surely you can decide for yourselves? Why is that one tree different? Is what you have really enough?'

As the voice grew louder inside, all I could think about was that one fruit. The others, which had tasted so full of flavour and been such a delight, seemed now to taste like dust. I became restless, returning constantly to look at it, standing gazing at it, imagining its delights. I would touch it, just briefly – after all, what harm could that do? At times I leant close enough to catch its aroma. I began to visualise eating it, rehearsing the fantasy, indulging my dream of how this one thing would make my life complete. It was my first thought on waking, my last as my eyelids drifted in sleep. I must have it. I must. I knew Eve felt the same.

Eve ate first, and I did not stop her. Instead, I took it too.

And everything was lost.

Genesis tells part of their story:

Now the snake was more crafty than any of the wild animals the LORD God had made. He said to the woman, 'Did God really say, "You must not eat from any tree in the garden"?'

The woman said to the snake, 'We may eat fruit from the trees in the garden, but God did say, "You must not eat fruit from the tree that is in the middle of the garden, and you must not touch it, or you will die."'

'You will not certainly die,' the snake said to the woman. 'For God knows that when you eat from it your eyes will be opened, and you will be like God, knowing good and evil.'

When the woman saw that the fruit of the tree was good for food and pleasing to the eye, and also desirable for gaining wisdom, she took some and ate it. She also gave some to her husband, who was with her, and he ate it. Then the eyes of both of them were opened, and they realised that they were naked; so they sewed fig leaves together and made coverings for themselves.

(Gen. 3:1–7)

Exploration of dissatisfaction

'(I Can't Get No) Satisfaction' is one of the world's most recognisable songs, first released by the Rolling Stones in the US in June 1965. It was not immediately released in the UK as the lyrics were thought too sexually suggestive, although the song talks equally about commercialism and the power of advertising. Arguably, marketing and the media have much to answer for in fueling dissatisfaction. Watching the apparently golden lives of others so easily becomes an incessant niggle: 'Why is my life not like that?' We see things we would not have thought we needed until they are paraded in front of us.

Finding satisfaction and contentment appears to be a deeply rooted human struggle. Many people dream of a lottery win, buying tickets faithfully week on week, and though some winners enjoy the easing of financial burdens, many find it does not bring them what they hoped for; indeed, it can be instead the cause of deep unhappiness.[1]

Satisfaction is when we receive or achieve something we want, need or hope for, such as when we are hungry and are satisfied by a meal. Let's begin by looking at the area of needs. The primary essential for every human being is to have enough of the basics to sustain life. In 1943, Abraham Maslow first published his 'hierarchy of needs' following his research into motivation. His theory was that we were motivated to meet the basic needs first before other less immediate essentials. In the language of this chapter, until the most basic needs are satisfied – in his pyramid, these are the physiological basics for food, water etc. – people will not be motivated to seek to fulfil the higher needs. He divides our requirements as people into five sections. Physiological, security/safety, love and belonging and self-esteem are all called deficiency needs – as we work through each of these, and they are met, we become motivated by the ultimate need, for self-actualisation, the realising of our full potential in every area and an acceptance of our limitations. As I write, there is a war in Ukraine. People in these extreme circumstances will be driven almost entirely by the first two – safety and physiological needs, although prior to the outbreak of hostilities they may have been highly motivated in the other areas. Maslow recognised that the journey through these needs would not be linear or once and for all, but that we would move between them during our lives, with some circumstances potentially taking us back to the 'lower' levels if our basic needs are under threat.

Christians vary in their attitude to the Adam and Eve story, but in terms of our exploration, it does not matter if the story is taken literally or seen as symbolic (Adam being Hebrew for 'man', Eve for 'woman'). The story suggests that at the beginning (and we can interpret this as in our early pre-natal development as individuals, in a wanted and healthy pregnancy, or historically as a species), our needs were fully met. In the garden story, certainly there was food, safety and security, and love and belonging, the latter needs met in relationship with firstly God, and then the other – Adam or Eve. What about self-esteem and self-actualisation? In the Genesis account it is said, 'The LORD God took the man and put him in the Garden of Eden to work it and take care of it.'[2] Sailhamer argues that a better translation of the specific Hebrew word would be 'to worship and obey' rather than to tend the ground.[3] In that case, it would appear that the 'higher' needs of self-esteem and self-actualisation were also met. Humanity could find fulfilment and satisfaction in the worship and service of God. In the Preface to *Toward a Psychology of Being*, Maslow outlines the difficulty some have had with the language of self-actualisation ('self' equating with selfish) and suggests the term 'full-humanness'.[4] Surely the Genesis account suggests that at the start, Adam and Eve – humanity – were fully and completely human, all that God intended, with every need satisfied. Was it their dissatisfaction, striving after autonomy and not being willing to answer to anyone else, which fractured the relationship with God? Does that remain true for us as individuals?

Returning to the earlier definition of satisfaction, it helps to remember that wishes and expectations are both very different from needs, and separate from each other. There may be things we wish, or desire, which may be helpful; for example, the desire to do well in studies or a career, which may help us strive to do our best. There are others which may be unhelpful to us, or even destructive, particularly if our reaching for them becomes overwhelming or obsessive – indeed, even a good thing can become damaging if it becomes our sole focus. Typing this, I definitely wish for a Magnum Double Raspberry ice cream (other makes and varieties are available!), but I do not need it. It is a wish which does not need to be satisfied, and I am better placed concentrating on what I am writing rather than salivating at the thought of it. Indeed, if I give it less mental space, I am likely to be less dissatisfied – or to put it another way, I need to put my thoughts elsewhere and be content with the cup of tea beside me instead, allowing the desire to fade into the background. Perhaps a helpful question to ask ourselves when faced with something we wish for is: 'Longer term, will this make me more human, more fully the person I was made to be? Is what I am wishing for a positive thing to seek, a neutral one, or something which could damage me?' That may help to decide if the desire is something which should be satisfied or not.

Expectations are different again. If I expect something, and that expectation is not met, then I will probably experience disappointment and dissatisfaction. If it is trivial, a meal in a restaurant which is not as good as it sounded on the menu for example, the feeling will not last. But if it is of more significance, such as a relationship which did not work out as I expected, the wounds can go much deeper. It is particularly difficult if my expectation was based on a felt or actual need. Insufficient love and acceptance in our early years can see us always seeking after those things in adulthood. The difficulty is that no one can replace parental love and our disappointment can turn to resentment towards those we believe have failed us. We need to face the reality of what we have not received, and grieve for it, rather than seek unhelpfully to replicate it.

More recent than Maslow's theories are those in the area of Life Satisfaction, and American psychologist Ed Diener created the Satisfaction With Life Scale (SWLS). Not surprisingly, life satisfaction is linked to the quality of our health, although interestingly, wisdom in older people, an understanding and acceptance of their lives, was equally important.[5] Life satisfaction is not the same as happiness, which is transient and very immediate. Rather it reflects our underlying basic position of contentment, or otherwise, with our lives.

Victor Frankl was a Jewish Austrian neurologist and psychiatrist who spent time in the concentration camps in the Second World War, where a number of his family, including his wife, died. After the war he wrote *Man's Search for Meaning*.[6] He believed that what makes people able to survive amid suffering is finding meaning and purpose. One aspect of this, he argued, is taking responsibility for our actions and choosing our attitude in any circumstances: surprisingly he found that those who gave away their rations actually survived longer than those who never shared. This taking of responsibility frees people, he maintained, to love, do meaningful work and endure suffering. Neither success nor happiness should be a goal, but love. Prisoners who showed love held on to hope, and it was the loss of hope that destroyed people. Adam and Eve did not take responsibility. In contrast Adam blamed Eve, and even God: 'The woman you put here with me – she gave me some fruit from the tree, and I ate it.'[7] Eve blames the snake. Humanity in general can be poor at taking responsibility, learning from an early age to shift blame elsewhere.

So how can we avoid a dissatisfaction that erodes our well-being? St Paul wrote in the letter to the Philippians that he had 'learned to be content whatever the circumstances'.[8]

This is an extraordinary statement from a man who elsewhere described the challenges his life and work had brought:

> Three times I was beaten with rods, once I was pelted with stones, three times I was shipwrecked, I spent a night and a day in the open sea, I have been constantly on the move. I have been in danger from rivers, in danger from bandits, in danger from my fellow Jews, in danger from Gentiles; in danger in the city, in danger in the country, in danger at sea; and in danger from false believers. I have laboured and toiled and have often gone without sleep; I have known hunger and thirst and have often gone without food; I have been cold and naked. Besides everything else, I face daily the pressure of my concern for all the churches.
>
> (2 Cor. 11:25–28)

How many of us, faced with those challenges, could say that we were content? For Paul, this was only possible 'through him who gives me strength'.[9] Paul had discovered the God of love, and found his own significance, and satisfaction, in serving him. Perhaps this can be our starting point too.

Reflection questions

- What are the things in your life that bring you satisfaction?
- Are there any areas where you are aware of dissatisfaction? What do you think might help you to come to terms with the difficulty that area presents?
- Are there any steps you need to take as a result of reflecting on this chapter?

Cain: Resentment

*Then the LORD said to Cain, 'Where is your
brother Abel?'
'I don't know,' he replied. 'Am I my brother's
keeper?'*

Gen. 4:9

The voice of Cain

I was the eldest, and that made me special. My mother always
said she saw me as a gift from God. A way to see something
good come from their new life, she said, to know the Maker
was still with them. Abel, he was just a second, a spare: mine
was to be the lineage. And my father showed me with pride
how to till the ground, his special calling from the beginning.
I worked hard, the crops were good. I took pleasure in produc-
ing what we needed.

We knew, somehow, that we needed to bring gifts to the
Maker. It was nothing that any of us voiced: it was simply a
knowledge within us, a form of hunger that we needed to satisfy.
I brought my precious plants first. Well, some of them. Abel
was quick to follow, from the firstborn of his flock. With no

idea how the lambing season would continue, he still brought the first, the best. Quick across my mind a thought flashed . . . was he trying to outdo me? How could he? He could never supplant my first place.

Yet, as time went on, he seemed to be blessed in a way I was not. His flocks flourished, and while the ground still yielded me produce, somehow it seemed more spindly, less generous than before. I kept working, harder and harder, a tinge of desperation creeping into the tasks I had previously enjoyed. Abel's animals grew ever stronger, and even my parents began to praise him for his husbandry. Their silence about my crops spoke volumes.

I began to feel angry. Why were things working so well for him? What had he done to deserve the Maker's blessing and why was it withheld from me? This nobody was not more worthy than I was. At first it was just a fleeting thought, a sense of unease in some dark recess of my mind, but it began to grow, and then fester like the rot that sometimes took over my crops when I neglected them. I found I could not dismiss the thought, but instead it became the front and centre of my waking life. Even seeing him, lamb across his shoulders, brought an eruption of anger. Why were good things coming to him? Why not me?

I began to lose interest in everything. A sourness began to stick in my throat. I snapped at my brother, who seemed bewildered at my change in attitude. We had never been close, but this sense of antipathy was new and I could sense his confusion. I somehow enjoyed harbouring my secret vitriol, the one thing in my life that was growing well.

Then one day, I sensed a nudge from the Maker. A questioning of my attitude – and I sensed a warning too, that an insidious force threatened to overwhelm me if I did not change.

But I was not willing. I had come to enjoy my sense of hurt outrage, holding it to me like a prized possession. I did not want to let it go, and then as time continued, it would not let *me* go. As the days dragged on, I hatched a plan. We would go walking, and finally I could release all my venom upon him, find a freedom from the internal prison I seemed to have found myself in. I would let my well-rehearsed speech spew from me and the poison be expunged. I would wound him with my words.

That was not what happened. He followed me like one of his trusting lambs, but when I opened the floodgates of my bitterness, mere words were not enough. Unthinking, with a hatred exploding from somewhere deep within, I picked up a rock and before I knew it, he was dead, his blood pooling on the ground around him like a silent rebuke.

And now I am a wanderer, and the Maker seems so far away.

Genesis tells part of his story:

Adam made love to his wife Eve, and she became pregnant and gave birth to Cain. She said, 'With the help of the LORD I have brought forth a man.' Later she gave birth to his brother Abel.

Now Abel kept flocks, and Cain worked the soil. In the course of time Cain brought some of the fruits of the soil as an offering to the LORD. But Abel also brought an offering – fat portions from some of the firstborn of his flock. The LORD looked with favour on Abel and his offering, but on Cain and his offering he did not look with favour. So Cain was very angry, and his face was downcast.

Then the LORD said to Cain, 'Why are you angry? Why is your face downcast? If you do what is right, will you not be accepted? But if you do not do what is right, sin is crouching at your door; it desires to have you, but you must rule over it.'

Now Cain said to his brother Abel, 'Let's go out to the field.'
While they were in the field, Cain attacked his brother Abel and
killed him.

Then the LORD said to Cain, 'Where is your brother Abel?'

'I don't know,' he replied. 'Am I my brother's keeper?'

The LORD said, 'What have you done? Listen! Your brother's
blood cries out to me from the ground. Now you are under a
curse and driven from the ground, which opened its mouth to
receive your brother's blood from your hand. When you work the
ground, it will no longer yield its crops for you. You will be a restless wanderer on the earth.'

(Gen. 4:1–12)

Exploration of resentment

All too easily, this story is seen as the ultimate case of sibling
rivalry, an adult and extreme version of the child who snatches
a toy from a younger one, or even pushes them in a moment
of toddler frustration. However, I don't think the story is quite
that simple. It is perhaps important, lest we dismiss it as not
relevant to us because we have no siblings, or a relationship
with them that does not give us these difficulties, not to lose
sight of the wider context. Let's take a closer look.

Resentment is an unpleasant feeling which we may experience if we have found ourselves in a situation we did not want
to be in, or believe we have been treated unjustly. This may be
something which has been done to us, or something we felt we
should have received and didn't. Cain felt that his offering was
not accepted and that he had been mistreated by God and perhaps too by his brother Abel. In the Bible account Abel is described, unlike Cain, by a throwaway line with no explanation

of his name, which actually means a puff of wind, something insignificant. The story leaves many questions open. Were their offerings different in quality? We are not told, although the phrase 'some of the fruits' might imply Cain's was less sacrificial, and God's later warning certainly implies that something in the offering was not right. We are also not told how they knew that one offering was accepted and the other not. What is clear is that the context is worship, rather than being brothers per se, and what follows indicates that it is what was happening in Cain's heart which was the issue.

In the best outcome, the frustration, disappointment or anger we feel as a very natural response to our distress and powerlessness in certain situations can be dealt with before it turns into resentment. However, if there is no apology or where there is a power imbalance, or other aspects which make the situation more complex, such as our own unhealed past, our initial response can turn inwards into a brooding bitterness. This is particularly the case if we struggle in general with expressing our emotions. At this stage, especially if we repeatedly revisit or rehearse the situation internally, it can damage both us and the relationships we have, particularly with anyone involved with the injustice. We may harbour a desire for revenge, which may be expressed either in passive aggression[1] or more directly. Cain was given a warning from God – an invitation to set his heart right. He needed to rule over his growing anger and resentment, but instead it mastered him, with violent repercussions.

Resentment can result from an experience which is no one's fault but still feels, or is, unfair, such as exhausted carers who can at times experience anger, which can become resentment even though they love the person they are caring for. That can be a very painful situation in which to try to keep our heart attitude a healthy one.

As we noted earlier, the context of the root of Cain's resentment was a situation of worship. Resentments towards others in church families can be difficult to admit to. Yet there are, aren't there, moments when, if we are ruthlessly honest, we have, however fleetingly, had negative thoughts about others around us in the church community? When we wonder why someone has a role we wanted, or is more recognised? When God seems to bless others, for example, answering their prayers when ours appear not to be? When some seem so gifted or popular and we feel overlooked or ordinary? There are also, of course, situations where we genuinely are mistreated by other Christians. Jesus was well aware of this possibility and gives us clear instructions, in a turn of phrase reminiscent of Cain's downfall: 'Therefore, if you are offering your gift at the altar and there remember that your brother or sister has something against you, leave your gift there in front of the altar. First go and be reconciled to them; then come and offer your gift.'[2]

Resentment can be difficult to deal with, but it is very important for our well-being to try to do so. A starting place is acknowledging the hurt which lies at the root rather than trying to deny it. We need to give it space and expression, voicing it to God with the same raw honesty we see in the Psalms. It may also help us to try to see the perspective of the other person, or a wider view of the situation. Abel had not sought to be blessed or for Cain not to be. We may be able to talk to the person concerned about our feelings, or if it is not possible or appropriate, to a trusted friend, church leader or counsellor, to unpack the origin of the buildup of resentment and have help letting it go and working on forgiveness – which can be a long process if the hurt is very deep.[3]

Reflection questions

- Have there been any times when you have felt you were treated unfairly?
- How were you able to resolve your feelings?
- If you are aware you still hold some resentment, what might be a possible next step to take?

3

Samson: Desire

> *Some time later, he fell in love with a woman in*
> *the Valley of Sorek whose name was Delilah.*
>
> Judg. 16:4

The voice of Samson

Here I am, grinding corn, just like the women, the sweet women, the love for whom has brought me here. I turn, and turn, my sightless eyes downcast, and I remember . . .

There have been four women in my life. The first gave me life, and I fear now, as I circle again and just catch the delicate aroma of the corn, that I have caused my mother pain. She was a wise woman, and a godly one. She named me after sunshine and for a time it must have been as though I brought that to her. Alas, no longer. I spurned her counsel, and that of my father. I knew best, it was what I wanted that counted. What did they know of the passion of youth, their bodies spent and dried?

Ah, the woman of Timnah! The second woman in my life and my first love. I can see her now still, as clear in my memory as she was to my sight that day. Her long hair glistened and how I loved that slim body. She turned to me, and the die was cast. I wanted her, and nothing was going to stand in my way. She was to be mine. My parents would need to arrange it, but it would be my choice, not theirs. I was going to have her.

My parents were horrified. They wanted me to find a woman from my own people, not a Philistine bride. Our people were enemies, but I cared nothing for the petty politics of the old ones. So we set off to make the arrangements. On the way, straying from the pathway to relieve myself, a young lion leapt towards me. I ripped it apart, scarcely thinking as I laid its body to the side of the path that I was betraying my Nazarite vow. But I said nothing. My parents would not have understood.

She was only my wife for a few days. That lion started a train of events which deprived me of my first love. She wept, she deceived me, telling my riddle, and she was given to another. My fury burned, and so did they. My revenge assuaged my pain and disappointment a little, but I still smouldered with disappointment and resentment.

Life settled for a time. I led the people, sorted their disputes and stayed within the boundaries of our territory. But then Gaza drew me again, like a moth lured to the flame of a camp fire. I paid this woman, the third, for her wares. She soothed the ache in my loins but not my heart. She meant nothing, and I was nearly trapped. For a time, I vowed to leave women alone. But then I met Delilah.

Delilah. How I loved her. What was it about those Philistine women? I never met their equal in my own people. The feel of her hair, her soft skin warmed by the sun. At last I would be happy, made complete in her arms, satiated by our love and at peace with myself. Finally I had the woman I wanted, the life I had yearned for. I would feel complete.

But it was not to be. At first, I was amused by her wanting to find the source of my strength. Three times I teased her, three times she played her foolish game. But she would not let it go, her begging chewing at my ear like a wild dog mithering the scraps. In the end, she looked at me, eyes wide and brimming with tears, saying I did not love her. I did, of course, I adored and worshipped her. And so I could resist her no more, and told her everything, including about the often-broken vow, and my hair.

I slept like a child in her lap. And she betrayed me.

The book of Judges tells part of his story:

Some time later, he fell in love with a woman in the Valley of Sorek whose name was Delilah. The rulers of the Philistines went to her and said, 'See if you can lure him into showing you the secret of his great strength and how we can overpower him so that we may tie him up and subdue him. Each one of us will give you eleven hundred shekels of silver.'

So Delilah said to Samson, 'Tell me the secret of your great strength and how you can be tied up and subdued.'

Samson answered her, 'If anyone ties me with seven fresh bow-strings that have not been dried, I'll become as weak as any other man.'

Then the rulers of the Philistines brought her seven fresh bow-strings that had not been dried, and she tied him with them. With men hidden in the room, she called to him, 'Samson, the Philistines are upon you!' But he snapped the bow-strings as easily as a piece of string snaps when it comes close to a flame. So the secret of his strength was not discovered.

Then Delilah said to Samson, 'You have made a fool of me; you lied to me. Come now, tell me how you can be tied.'

He said, 'If anyone ties me securely with new ropes that have never been used, I'll become as weak as any other man.'

So Delilah took new ropes and tied him with them. Then, with men hidden in the room, she called to him, 'Samson, the Philistines are upon you!' But he snapped the ropes off his arms as if they were threads.

Delilah then said to Samson, 'All this time you have been making a fool of me and lying to me. Tell me how you can be tied.'

He replied, 'If you weave the seven braids of my head into the fabric on the loom and tighten it with the pin, I'll become as weak as any other man.' So while he was sleeping, Delilah took the seven braids of his head, wove them into the fabric and tightened it with the pin.

Again she called to him, 'Samson, the Philistines are upon you!' He awoke from his sleep and pulled up the pin and the loom, with the fabric.

Then she said to him, 'How can you say, "I love you," when you won't confide in me? This is the third time you have made a fool of me and haven't told me the secret of your great strength.' With such nagging she prodded him day after day until he was sick to death of it.

So he told her everything. 'No razor has ever been used on my head,' he said, 'because I have been a Nazirite dedicated to God from my mother's womb. If my head were shaved, my strength would leave me, and I would become as weak as any other man.'

When Delilah saw that he had told her everything, she sent word to the rulers of the Philistines, 'Come back once more; he has told me everything.' So the rulers of the Philistines returned with the silver in their hands. After putting him to sleep on her lap, she called for someone to shave off the seven braids of his hair, and so began to subdue him. And his strength left him.

Then she called, 'Samson, the Philistines are upon you!' He awoke from his sleep and thought, 'I'll go out as before and shake myself free.' But he did not know that the LORD had left him.

Then the Philistines seized him, gouged out his eyes and took him down to Gaza. Binding him with bronze shackles, they set him to grinding corn in the prison.

(Judg. 16:4–21. See also 13:1 – 16:4; 16:22–31)

Exploration of desire

The concept of 'desire' has had a complex history within Christian circles, being equated all too readily with sexual desire, indeed with lust, one of the seven deadly sins.[1] Desire has been seen as something to be eliminated or at least kept in check. Certainly, there is no doubt that at times acting on our desires can have disastrous results, as the unrestrained expression of both sexual desires and those related to anger and revenge in the life of Samson demonstrates.

Perhaps another basis for the attitude of hostility or at best ambivalence towards the place of desires in Christian teaching is that desires are more easily associated with this present earthly existence, which seems so real and tangible, rather than a more mysterious look ahead to eternity. Yet to be human is to have desires: for example, we are born with an innate need to satisfy our hunger. Perhaps it is the type of desire, or what we do with it, that is the more fundamental issue. We need to take a more nuanced view.

Desire suggests a wanting, or even more strongly a craving, for something we do not have or do not possess enough of, which we believe will do us good or bring us pleasure. Some may be able to be obtained by our actions and others are, if only temporarily, beyond our grasp. If we desire a cup of tea, then assuming we are at home or near a tea shop, we can satisfy that desire with relative ease. However, if we desire a million-pound house, that is not a yearning most of us can satisfy. The fulfilment of some desires may lie within the power of others to grant us, for example, a job we might really want, which the interview panel could give us. Samson's desire for the woman at Timnah was reliant on his parents accepting his decision and negotiating the marriage. Some desires are fulfilled within themselves, others are a step towards a deeper or bigger aspiration – such as a better job which may help me obtain a foot on the housing ladder. Others are simply not possible at all, however much we might long for them – back to that million-pound house. In that case, our challenge is what to do with the desire in order to prevent us becoming dissatisfied or resentful.[2]

At times, desires are based on a legitimate need – such as our thirst leading us to drink water. At other times the basis is want, not need, although it can be difficult at times to distinguish between the two.[3] Marketing and advertising seek to persuade us that something we want is actually a need, to entice us to purchase the item or service. The products for sale are linked with something the consumer desires, such as beauty, health, or a particular lifestyle, and are designed in a way to convince us that our life will be enhanced with it, and by implication diminished without.

The complexity of an apparently simple word such as desire is exemplified in the number of theories that surround it. The first are action-based theories, based on the principle that a desire will lead us towards action, although not every circumstance will allow that action to take place. However, not every desire will result in action, and we may not achieve what we hope for:

as Paul expressed it, 'For I do not do the good I want to do, but the evil I do not want to do – this I keep on doing.'[4] The second set of theories are the pleasure-based theories of desire, which as the title implies are based around the principle that the desires we have derive from actual or anticipated enjoyment and satisfaction. The next set are good-based theories, where desire is rooted in our perception of what is good – not necessarily used in a moral sense. There are attention-based theories – what is it that draws us to attend to certain things and so find them desirable? Learning-based theories suggest a link between learning, reward and desire. If we are rewarded for our learning, we desire it, and the things which facilitate it, more. Finally, there are holistic theories, which take a broader view with the potential for multiple facets to desire. All of these theories have proponents and detractors:[5] desire is not as straightforward as we might think.

At any one time, a number of desires will be present within us. Some may be strong, feeling almost irresistible, and at the forefront of our minds. I strongly want to finish this chapter today, and it is very much part of my consciousness, while other desires, such as for food, are less so at present but may assume a greater strength later. Our desires too may at times be kept in check for the good of society or others. For example, our desire to acquire wealth, status or other things is not pursued in order to allow us to serve others with our giving or service, perhaps taking a lower paid or less visible role. As parents we overcome the desire for sleep to tend to a hungry new-born or a sick older child.

The, at times, negative attitude in Christian circles to desire is, as stated earlier, because it is often associated with sexual desire. Most people would acknowledge that the outworking in behaviour of unrestrained sexual desire can be damaging.

However, the Bible does not have a negative attitude to sexual desire in itself. Rather it is seen as a good, God-given gift in the context of a loving relationship. However we interpret the Song of Songs – as a straightforward love poem or a metaphor for God's love – it contains within it celebratory sensual language. We might argue the same about the desire for power. The exercise of power can, of course, be damaging. However, Paul prays for the Ephesians '. . . that the eyes of your heart may be enlightened in order that you may know the hope to which he has called you, the riches of his glorious inheritance in his holy people, and his incomparably great power for us who believe. That power is the same as the mighty strength he exerted when he raised Christ from the dead . . .'.[6] We are encouraged to desire power from the Holy Spirit to live out our Christian lives.

The Christian writer Henri Nouwen points out that desire is often portrayed as something to be subdued in us, yet encourages us to see that while some desires (or perhaps in particular any resulting actions) can be troublesome, others can be worthy and important. He encourages us to see the desire for God as what should root us, enabling us to judge the appropriateness of the other things we yearn for, and to use spiritual disciplines to keep our desires helpful rather than destructive.[7] At the end of his life Samson, though still flawed, seeks God in a final prayer.[8] His weaknesses and mistakes do not stop him being listed in Hebrews 11 as one of the heroes of faith.[9] There is hope for us all.

The New Testament is balanced in its approach. The desire to care for ourselves, for example, is not seen as intrinsically wrong or selfish. Jesus encourages us to love our neighbour as ourselves,[10] which assumes that we do care for or look after ourselves, and Paul's teaching of our bodies as the temple of the

Holy Spirit has a double edge: both to resist unhelpful desires which might result in sexual immorality, which was his context, but surely also to cherish and care for our bodies in a healthy way?[11] Equally, we are instructed to practise self-sacrifice, the denial perhaps of some desires, in our Christian discipleship: 'Whoever does not take up their cross and follow me is not worthy of me. Whoever finds their life will lose it, and whoever loses their life for my sake will find it.'[12] We would do well to be aware of our desires, healthy and less so, obvious and hidden, and see how we can harness them for our growth and for the kingdom.

Reflection questions

- Think back over your day today. What desires are you aware of? Are they helpful or unhelpful, fulfilled or unfulfilled?
- How strong is your desire to seek God and live for him? Be honest!
- What does it mean when the psalmist writes: 'Take delight in the LORD, and he will give you the desires of your heart'?[13]

Ruth: Loyalty

But Ruth replied, 'Don't urge me to leave you or to turn back from you. Where you go I will go, and where you stay I will stay. Your people will be my people and your God my God. Where you die I will die, and there I will be buried. May the LORD deal with me, be it ever so severely, if even death separates you and me.'

Ruth 1:16–17

The voice of Ruth

I can pinpoint the exact moment I knew I would stay with Naomi, and be there for her whatever it took. We were burying my brother-in-law Kilion, and this time, although sad, I was not as distraught as when we were putting my beloved Mahlon to rest just a few months before. Instead I was supporting my sister, holding her up as she wept. As I did so, just for a moment I glimpsed Naomi. She was not crying, but simply staring at the ground where we had just laid the second of her sons, beside the grave of her husband. There was such an emptiness about her, as though the very life had been sucked from her and all that remained was a shell, with nothing at the core. As profound as my own grief was, I could not imagine hers – to lose a husband and both sons, the future bleak with no one to provide for her, to protect her.

It had taken me a while to understand Naomi and Elimelek, while he lived. Their strange God, Yahweh, was the only one they served and seemed nothing like our god Chemosh and the other gods we worshipped. We are a proud nation, as are they. I understood them coming to us in a time of famine, though I wondered why they did not trust their God to help them. At first there was suspicion – our nations have always had friction – but in the end our common humanity won over and when Orpah and I married Kilion and Mahlon we accepted each other, especially recognising how hard it was for Naomi with her husband gone.

But now her sons had left us too, and she looked empty and spent, like a husk which has no purpose once the seeds are blown away on the wind. I knew from that moment at their graves that I would support and take care of her, both from the love that had grown in me for her and for the sake of her son with whom I had hoped to spend so many more years.

But then she said she was going home. There was food there now, she told us, and it was where she belonged. Through a long, sleepless night I agonised over it, and cried too, because I knew I needed to go with her, but the cost lay heavily on my heart. My grief would have been easier to bear in my home country with all that was familiar. To leave with her freely and lovingly and not grudgingly, either then or later, meant a new life away from my other family, my friends, and everything that I had known. I would need to abandon my gods for their one God, yet something in their devotion to Yahweh had drawn me even before this heartache and I sensed that this might be the easiest of all the prices to pay.

I told Orpah of my decision, and at first she said she would come too. Yet when it came to it Naomi tried to send us both back. She was despairing, and angry too at her God, despite her worship of him. She saw no hope for our futures if we returned with her. So Orpah turned back, and I was sad to see her go but determined to see my decision through. No matter what it took, no matter what the future held, I would stay with Naomi. The die was cast, the vow made, and we were going to head into an unknown future together.

The book of Ruth tells part of her story:

In the days when the judges ruled, there was a famine in the land. So a man from Bethlehem in Judah, together with his wife and two sons, went to live for a while in the country of Moab. The man's name was Elimelek, his wife's name was Naomi, and the names of his two sons were Mahlon and Kilion. They were Ephrathites from Bethlehem, Judah. And they went to Moab and lived there.

Now Elimelek, Naomi's husband, died, and she was left with her two sons. They married Moabite women, one named Orpah and the other Ruth. After they had lived there about ten years, both Mahlon and Kilion also died, and Naomi was left without her two sons and her husband.

When Naomi heard in Moab that the LORD had come to the aid of his people by providing food for them, she and her daughters-in-law prepared to return home from there. With her two daughters-in-law she left the place where she had been living and set out on the road that would take them back to the land of Judah.

Then Naomi said to her two daughters-in-law, 'Go back, each of you, to your mother's home. May the LORD show you kindness, as you have shown kindness to your dead husbands and to me. May the LORD grant that each of you will find rest in the home of another husband.' Then she kissed them goodbye and they wept aloud and said to her, 'We will go back with you to your people.'

But Naomi said, 'Return home, my daughters. Why would you come with me? Am I going to have any more sons, who could become your husbands? Return home, my daughters; I am too old to have another husband. Even if I thought there was still hope for me – even if I had a husband tonight and then gave birth to sons – would you wait until they grew up? Would you remain unmarried for them? No, my daughters. It is more bitter for me than for you, because the LORD's hand has turned against me!'

At this they wept aloud again. Then Orpah kissed her mother-in-law goodbye, but Ruth clung to her.

'Look,' said Naomi, 'your sister-in-law is going back to her people and her gods. Go back with her.'

But Ruth replied, 'Don't urge me to leave you or to turn back from you. Where you go I will go, and where you stay I will stay. Your people will be my people and your God my God. Where you die I will die, and there I will be buried. May the LORD deal with me, be it ever so severely, if even death separates you and me.' When Naomi realised that Ruth was determined to go with her, she stopped urging her.

(Ruth 1:1–18; see also the remainder of the book)

Exploration of loyalty

I wonder what comes to your mind when you hear the word 'loyalty'? There are several possibilities: the supermarket loyalty card in your pocket, a friend or, perhaps, an example of disloyalty you have experienced.

Loyalty is the feeling, and resulting behaviour, which occurs when through personal relationship or other attachment, such as is formed in a work setting, we offer support or allegiance to a person, institution, or cause. Interestingly much more is written and research conducted about both loyalty in business and maintaining a customer base, and loyalty to a country, than loyalty in personal relationships, even though it can be argued that because loyalty is a personal, relational quality it is only true loyalty in human interactions, not commercial ones. It is only genuinely tested when there is a cost to maintaining it – as there certainly would have been for Ruth, leaving her homeland, with all that entailed, for a completely new life. We know that the story has a good ending, but she did not have at the time the benefit of hindsight which we possess.

Loyalty is a more complex quality than it might appear at first, and related to other aspects of our emotional lives. Loyalty and trust, for example, are closely linked. Generally speaking, we only give loyalty to individuals or institutions which we trust, and may cease to be loyal if that trust is broken or damaged in some way. In contrast, loyalty from fear is not likely to be fully genuine. As mentioned previously, as I write there is a war in Ukraine. Soldiers of any country who are kept 'loyal' from fear of punishment are less likely to be truly loyal than those who are not under threat but fighting from duty to, or even love of, their country.

The capacity for loyalty is also linked to the ability to form consistent attachments, which as research by British psychologist John Bowlby and others has demonstrated, is very dependent on our experiences of caregivers in childhood.[1] Where an attachment is not strong, loyalty may well not be either.

Perhaps this link with attachment may explain the occasional stories in which animals appear to show what we might otherwise assume is the exclusively human quality of loyalty. One of the most well-known is 'Greyfriars Bobby', a terrier who is supposed to have spent fourteen years guarding the grave of his master. We might well see the apparent 'loyalty' of animals as mercenary loyalty (see below), but this and other similar stories leave some questions unanswered.

Loyalty is also complicated by the fact that we have the capacity to be loyal, which is seen as a virtue and a positive quality, to something which is destructive or even evil. The fact that someone or something inspires loyalty in others does not in itself make them or it worthy or moral. In such instances something else other than the laudable nature of the object of the loyalty is at work.

Author Rajat Paharia[2] lists in his book four different levels of loyalty which, although written in a business context, can have a broader application. First on his list is inertia loyalty – not having the time or energy to look for another firm or brand. It was interesting that during the pandemic a number of people, perhaps finding they had a little more time, made moves to different churches. Anecdotally there was a mixture of reasons. Some were linked to major moves or life changes of other kinds, but others used the opportunity while the churches were not gathering in person, making it easier to leave as, perhaps, loyalty was weakened. The next is mercenary loyalty – in a business context because of points or other rewards. Perhaps we do stay loyal because of what we get out of a church or relationship, or conversely leave when we feel our needs are not being met, but certainly in Ruth's case this was not the motivation.

Naomi was, by her own admission, bitter and would not have been the easiest person to accompany. Ruth's loyalty to her would have involved considerable personal resilience. The third kind Paharia lists is true loyalty – an emotional connection. We can surmise, surely, that this was so for Ruth. The history of shared family life and indeed of their mutual grief had clearly cemented their bond. The fourth level Paharia lists is cult loyalty – where the person or object to which we are loyal is linked with our values or identity – as we see, for example, in followers of a sports team. Ruth's loyalty to Naomi, in contrast, actually cost her the loyalty to her own tribe and people.

Loyalty as a word is found very infrequently in the Bible and not at all in the New Testament. Yet the teaching of Jesus does warn about the difficulty of divided loyalties: 'No one can serve two masters. Either you will hate the one and love the other, or you will be devoted to the one and despise the other.'[3] While that teaching is in the context of not loving both God and money, it would certainly hold true in other examples of mixed loyalties, as James writes: 'Therefore, anyone who chooses to be a friend of the world becomes an enemy of God.'[4] The strong image of the church as family with the many commands to care for one another, while not explicitly mentioning loyalty, certainly implies the need for it among Christians: 'in Christ we, though many, form one body, and each member belongs to all the others.'[5]

The story of Ruth reminds us that loyalty may well have results which we could not possibly foresee. How different might the genealogy of Jesus have been had she turned back when Naomi asked her?[6] God used the loyalty of this remarkable woman in his wider purposes – perhaps this may be the case in our lives too.

Reflection questions

- Where do you feel that your primary loyalty lies at this point in your life?
- Have you ever experienced disloyalty – either being disloyal or receiving it from someone or something?
- Have your loyalties changed over the years and in what way?

Eli's sons: Greed

Eli's sons were scoundrels; they had no regard for the LORD.

1 Sam. 2:12

The voice of Eli

I am old. I am tired. And I have failed.

A man of God came to see me today and told me, eyes clear and gaze unrelenting, what I already knew. Even in my love for my sons I have failed them. I have let them take paths that have disgraced the family and dishonoured God. But he did not stop there. He told me my line was to end, and my sons are to die, together and on the same day. I am utterly crushed. There is nothing for me now but the decline of the years until I join my ancestors, whose good name I have also betrayed. I am watching my sons' lives go to ruin and I can do nothing. I have tried to tell them, implored them, to no avail. It is all too late.

What makes my shame so much deeper, is that I have no one else to blame. I am their father, and I have let them down. Perhaps if their mother had still been alive, it might have been different. But no, I cannot escape my duty in that way. It was my responsibility, mine alone, to bring them up in God's ways, to show them that the priesthood is an honour and not an opportunity for greed and opportunism. That God is merciful but also just, that his compassion is not to be presumed upon and scorned. I too have eaten at the table supplied by their sin.

So I sit here at the doorpost of Shiloh, my beloved Shiloh, and remember how I learned at my father's knee to serve God. My mind drifts back over the years, the reminiscences sharp with regret, recalling how I had tried to do the same for my sons. I was so proud that they would carry on the priestly line, and their sons too, I hoped. In my arrogance I took so much for granted. I missed the signs that their love was for what they could gain and not for God. Did I not seek him enough? Did I love my position and the family name more than God? I have so many questions.

I hear Samuel approaching. He will be God's choice. For me, everything is finished, and in ruins.

The book of 1 Samuel tells part of their story:

Eli's sons were scoundrels; they had no regard for the LORD. Now it was the practice of the priests that, whenever any of the people offered a sacrifice, the priest's servant would come with a three-pronged fork in his hand while the meat was being boiled and would plunge the fork into the pan or kettle or cauldron or pot. Whatever the fork brought up the priest would take for himself. This is how they treated all the Israelites who came to Shiloh. But even before the fat was burned, the priest's servant would come and say to the person who was sacrificing, 'Give the priest some meat to roast; he won't accept boiled meat from you, but only raw.'

If the person said to him, 'Let the fat be burned first, and then take whatever you want,' the servant would answer, 'No, hand it over now; if you don't, I'll take it by force.'

This sin of the young men was very great in the LORD's sight, for they were treating the LORD's offering with contempt.

(1 Sam. 2:12–17. See also verses 27–36; 1 Sam. 4)

Exploration of greed

We tend to associate greed with an overconsumption of food, yet it is actually simply to want more of anything than we need, including food but also money. We might want to add possessions, status, power, or even experiences; anything for which we can crave more than we need. We find ourselves asking the question: when does need become greed?

In the case of Eli's sons, the area where they initially went wrong is food, although perhaps that was the symptom of a deeper malaise. After sacrifices had been made at Shiloh, when meat was being cooked by the often poor families who had brought the offering, the priest's servant could put a fork into the pot, and what was brought out could go to the priest by way of payment. Eli's sons were demanding, via the servant, meat to be taken before the offering, so that they had bigger portions which could then be roasted, and depriving the family both of presenting their sacrifice to God in the prescribed way, and of much-needed food.

Their rebellion went deeper, however, as they were also engaged in sexual relationships with the women who served at the entrance to Shiloh. These two men were the opposite of all that priestly ministry stood for – self-seeking rather than sacrificial, serving their appetites rather than God. In the end they became involved in a peculiar scheme involving the ark which ended in disaster – their lives were lost and the ark was captured. More tragedy followed as Eli died when he heard the news and Phinehas's wife also died, in childbirth, her labour hastened by the news of her husband's death. Her dying bequest to her son was to give him the name Ichabod, meaning 'no glory'. The story of Eli's sons has a catastrophic ending. Their greed and rebellion brought disaster on their family.

We may infer from Eli's assumption in 1 Samuel 1 that Hannah was drunk[1] that there was a general atmosphere of self-indulgence at the time, including around the worship at Shiloh. Societies and communities where self-indulgence is prevalent have, of course, always existed and warnings against greed come in many forms across literature and mythology. One of the most well-known of these is the story of Midas. He was offered any reward he chose, and opted for asking that everything he touched turned to gold. Initial delight turned to horror when he realised it was a curse and not a blessing. So what lies at the heart of greed? What can we learn from it?

It is important before looking at greed to separate it from addiction. Addiction is a recognised illness[2] where the sufferer has genuinely lost control over the ability to stop taking a substance or indulging in other behaviour which is harmful to them. Often the initial satisfaction or 'high' wanes and so the amount needed to satisfy the craving becomes greater and greater. The addiction may be physical – such as with various drugs – or emotional, such as an addiction to work or the internet, or a combination of both physical and psychological. Studies suggest quite a high genetic predisposition to addiction in addition to environmental factors.[3] Self-help groups such as Alcoholics Anonymous can be helpful and some professional resources are available, though the path to recovery is demanding and relapses can be common.

Greed, however, is different from addiction. Last night our grandchildren were with us and I had baked them a cake. As someone who battles my weight, I took a tiny piece and ate it. The next piece I had a moment later was, if I'm honest, self-indulgence. Greed is complex and has at least two roots. The first is physical. A number of substances, including foods, increase dopamine levels. Dopamine is a neurotransmitter, one of the chemicals which transmit signals between nerve cells in the brain. It influences the pleasure centre of the brain, affecting mood. Reaching for the chocolate (or, interestingly, cheese, due to its fat content) when we need a boost does have a physical basis. There is early research that suggests there may be a link between obesity and impaired dopamine pathways.[4] A number of foods help release dopamine, some of which are healthier than others. The difficulty with fast foods is they do cause a spike in dopamine production, but this is followed by a crash, starting a vicious circle. Add the tendency of parents to comfort distressed children with food (continuing from feeding a crying infant who may not be hungry), and the power of advertising (I went to the cinema recently and all the advertisements bar one were for food) and it is a powerful mix.

Another root for greed is emotional. If we do not receive the care we need in our early years, through inconsistent care, trauma or abuse, we can deal with the resulting feelings of loss and anger by seeking a substitute to fill the gap. The owning of a luxury item becomes linked with a sense of worth and self-esteem. However, if the need we are trying to fill is emotional and actually one that should have been met much earlier, whatever possessions we obtain or achievements we attain, it will never be enough. It is similar to the more extreme difficulty of hoarding which is a recognised disorder with psychological roots.[5] Food may be a particular difficulty here as it is so strongly linked in our unconscious memories with nurture. There is a marked absence of mention of Eli's wife, the mother to Hophni and Phinehas, in contrast to Hannah's story which precedes theirs, and so we can only guess what part, if any, she played in their upbringing and the kind of care they received.

These individual experiences will vary enormously, but alongside our specific life histories lies the more general existential anxiety which, as far as we can tell, is unique to human beings. At some point in our upbringings, we become aware of our mortality. I was brought up in a hospital as my father worked there and we lived in the grounds. Together with the natural surroundings, not least the impact of the severe winter of 1962–63, known as the Big Freeze, on the wildlife around me, I was aware of death from a very early age. Whether in our younger years or later, we become aware of the limit of our lifespan in a way which, it appears, animals are not. Perhaps greed, which also does not seem prevalent in animals or birds unless humans overfeed them and create a habit problem, is in part a reaction to the awareness that our time is limited and we need to cram things in – sometimes literally. It becomes a way of shielding ourselves from realities we do not wish to face.

The New Testament concentrates in particular on greed in relation to money. In the West we have arguably an ambivalent attitude to it – envying the life of the wealthy yet resenting institutions we see as grasping or benefiting financially from the distress of others. When Jesus was asked to arbitrate over an inheritance, he gave a stark warning to the gathered crowd: 'Watch out! Be on your guard against all kinds of greed; life does not consist in an abundance of possessions.'[6] The letter to Timothy contains the well-known though often misquoted phrase, 'For the love of money is a root of all kinds of evil.'[7] The Greek word literally means 'hankering after'. The next phrase in the NIV is: 'Some people, eager for money, have wandered from the faith and pierced themselves with many griefs' – in the RSV the phrase is the 'craving' for money. The Pharisees are described as loving money,[8] and Hebrews 13:5 is direct: 'Keep your lives free from the love of money and be content with what you have'. Greed and gluttony both appear in the list of 'deadly sins'. In stark contrast one aspect of the fruit of the Spirit is described as 'self-control'.[9] Although some types and expressions of asceticism have been unhealthy, the New Testament speaks clearly about the need for discipline, under-pinned always by God's grace.[10]

When does the healthy desire to meet practical needs, do well in work, provide for ourselves and our families and enjoy pleasurable aspects of our lives tip into greed? Perhaps that is a decision only we can make with some honest reflection, and so that is where we turn next – with some questions to consider.

Reflection questions

- How easy do you find it to exercise self-discipline?
- Are there particular areas of your life that are more of a struggle than others?
- What role models have you had of a life which is disciplined?

David: Mercy

> *Mephibosheth bowed down and said, 'What is*
> *your servant, that you should notice a dead dog*
> *like me?'*
>
> 2 Sam. 9:8

The voice of Mephibosheth

This is it. David has sent for me. As the new king, he will kill us all. There will be no mercy for me, carrying as I do Saul's blood within my veins. It is the moment I have dreaded for years, beginning with the hazy memories of my nurse snatching me from my bed as I slept, and the fear and panic around me which I could not understand but which somehow seeped into my very soul. I can still recall the pain I felt as we fell, as though my whole body, head to toe, was screaming in agony. And later the slow, terrible realisation that I would never walk properly, never run freely, again. I hated seeing my nurse's tears, shed so often as she watched me over the months, her regret and constant apologies doing nothing to ease how I felt. We heard so many stories told about David in our new life, as we hid in no man's land, my kingly ancestry meaning nothing except a secret to be kept lest I become a target for David or his followers.

And now, my miserable life is to be ended. I am bowing in front of the king, unable to meet his eyes. There will be such hatred there. My grandfather was cold-blooded in his pursuit of David, I have been told. Aside from the enmity that lay between them, new kings always purge the families of the old regime in a brutal bid to preserve the new. It is just how it is.

Absorbed in my misery, bowing as best I can amid my usual discomfort in standing on my injured legs, it takes me a moment to realise. He has called me by name. By name! Somehow even in my misery I catch his tone. Not harsh and hateful, as I expected, but gentle, compassionate even. And then the most extraordinary words: 'Don't be afraid'? Terrified is all I have ever been, for as long as I can remember. Could this encounter really be any different? I dare not hope.

If hearing my name was a shock, how much more so are these words which follow. I had heard that David and my father, Jonathan, had been friends, but I had never dreamt that their bond would be honoured in such a way. The king is speaking of kindness, but much more than that, of restitution, restoration; that he will return my grandfather's lands – my rightful inheritance, but one I never expected to receive.

The final part of his offering is the most shocking of all. A place at his table, royal protection and provision. Suddenly I feel overwhelmed. Why is he doing this? I am a nothing, a nobody. From scrimping a meagre living, now I will have the proceeds of my grandfather's land, and my family, my precious son, can be properly provided for. I am spared, but so much more than that. Instead of death, I am offered life. Where I expected judgement, there is surprising mercy. Finally, I have hope for the future.

2 Samuel 9 tells part of his story:

David asked, 'Is there anyone still left of the house of Saul to whom I can show kindness for Jonathan's sake?'

Now there was a servant of Saul's household named Ziba. They summoned him to appear before David, and the king said to him, 'Are you Ziba?'

'At your service,' he replied.

The king asked, 'Is there no one still alive from the house of Saul to whom I can show God's kindness?'

Ziba answered the king, 'There is still a son of Jonathan; he is lame in both feet.' 'Where is he?' the king asked.

Ziba answered, 'He is at the house of Makir son of Ammiel in Lo Debar.'

So King David had him brought from Lo Debar, from the house of Makir son of Ammiel.

When Mephibosheth son of Jonathan, the son of Saul, came to David, he bowed down to pay him honour.

David said, 'Mephibosheth!'

'At your service,' he replied.

'Don't be afraid,' David said to him, 'for I will surely show you kindness for the sake of your father Jonathan. I will restore to you all the land that belonged to your grandfather Saul, and you will always eat at my table.'

Mephibosheth bowed down and said, 'What is your servant, that you should notice a dead dog like me?'

Then the king summoned Ziba, Saul's steward, and said to him, 'I have given your master's grandson everything that belonged to Saul and his family. You and your sons and your servants are to farm the land for him and bring in the crops, so that your master's grandson may be provided for. And Mephibosheth, grandson of your master, will always eat at my table.' (Now Ziba had fifteen sons and twenty servants.)

Then Ziba said to the king, 'Your servant will do whatever my lord the king commands his servant to do.' So Mephibosheth ate at David's table like one of the king's sons.

Mephibosheth had a young son named Mika, and all the members of Ziba's household were servants of Mephibosheth. And Mephibosheth lived in Jerusalem, because he always ate at the king's table; he was lame in both feet.

(2 Sam. 9:1–13. See also 2 Sam. 4:4)

Exploration of mercy

There are a number of definitions of mercy, many of which refer to showing compassion or forgiveness to those over whom the person has power. This was certainly the case for Mephibosheth as he stood before David in this remarkable and heartwarming story. These were very different and harsher times. Particularly given the difficult and stormy time David had experienced to establish his reign, the normal pattern would have been that he would execute any remaining members of his predecessor Saul's family to ensure there were no contenders left who would attempt to seize back the throne. David's question, 'Is there anyone still left of the house of Saul to whom I can show kindness for Jonathan's sake?' would have been a totally unexpected one to those around him. Mephibosheth would undoubtedly never have imagined he would receive mercy from David. He would have been unaware of Jonathan's request to David many years before to 'not ever cut off your kindness from my family – not even when the LORD has cut off every one of David's enemies from the face of the earth.'[1] David honours this in not only sparing Mephibosheth but going further by treating him with generosity and honour.

Jonathan's request was born out of David and Jonathan's deep love for each other, but David had earlier shown mercy in a relationship governed by enmity. 1 Samuel 24 relates how David had the perfect opportunity to kill Saul, whose jealousy had led him to hunt David down in an attempt to kill him, when Saul entered a cave to relieve himself. David instead crept into the cave and cut a segment off Saul's robe, though later, respecting Saul's position despite their history, he regretted even having done that.[2] When he told Saul of his actions, Saul was moved by David's mercy and there was (sadly only temporarily) peace between them. David later himself needed God's mercy after his catastrophic moral failure in committing adultery with Bathsheba and then murdering her husband to try to disguise it. In Psalm 51, written after this catastrophe, he cries out for forgiveness: 'Have mercy on me, O God, according to your unfailing love; according to your great compassion blot out my transgressions.'[3] Other psalms too, some of them written by David and used in worship by Jews and Christians alike across the millennia, speak frequently of, and cry out for, God's mercy.

Mercy is a huge biblical theme: indeed, in some ways it would be possible to argue that it is the primary one. At the start of the biblical account, after their disobedience, while Adam and Eve still need to face the consequences of their actions, God clothes them, covering their shame.[4] When Moses asks to see God's glory, he is reminded of his mercy.[5] Although God's people repeatedly rebel, and likewise suffer the repercussions, still God shows them mercy, reaching out to them again and again through the prophets. Supremely this mercy

at the heart of God is demonstrated in the life, death and resurrection of Jesus. There are many examples in the gospels of
people begging Jesus to show them mercy: the tax collector
from Jesus' story, the ten lepers, and blind Bartimaeus[6] are just
three instances. Peter's calling to discipleship is founded on his
recognition of his need for mercy,[7] and after the resurrection
he receives both mercy and a new commission despite having
denied knowing Jesus three times.[8]

One of the most moving examples from the life of Jesus is
his treatment of the woman caught in adultery.[9] Too immersed
in her shame to ask Jesus for anything, she nonetheless received
mercy despite the inability of her captors to offer her anything
other than scorn and judgement. What a contrast in her experience from Jesus, to the ruthless treatment of Monica Lewinsky
in the wake of her affair with President Bill Clinton.[10] Jesus,
in the consistency of his compassion, personified what the
writer of Lamentations had discovered: that there is an endless,
ever-renewed supply of the mercy of God.[11] Paul, who as a
persecutor of the early church had himself experienced God's
mercy, also recognised this quality as at the core of who God
is.[12] So we too can 'approach God's throne of grace with confidence, so that we may receive mercy and find grace to help us
in our time of need'.[13]

As we have seen, there are frequent references in the Bible to
God's mercy, but a proportion of the verses concerning mercy
are instead in relation to the mercy we need to show one another. Flowing from the very centre of God's identity, there is
an expectation that following God means that we will ourselves
exercise mercy. Mercy is different from pity, which implies su-
periority, or distance. Mercy comes from compassion, feeling
for and standing with the other person in their need. It also
implies that we do not only cultivate an attitude, but also take

action. We may feel compassion, or the desire to be merciful, but until it is demonstrated in the attitudes we hold and the resulting behaviours, it is not truly mercy. The Old Testament prophets recognised that this quality was more important than potentially meaningless rituals. Hosea, who had exemplified mercy in the difficult calling of his personal life, came to recognise that God requires 'mercy, not sacrifice, and acknowledgment of God rather than burnt offerings'[14] and Micah summarises what God requires of us as to 'act justly and to love mercy and to walk humbly with your God'.[15] The nature of these actions will vary: sometimes they will be practical acts of kindness, such as were exemplified in the life and work of Mother Teresa among many others. Often, to live in the light of this command will involve exercising forgiveness, a complex issue we will return to in a later chapter with the story of Stephen. A starting point to the costly and sometimes lengthy journey of forgiveness is both to recognise our own need for forgiveness and to be willing to begin that journey.

Jesus made clear in his teaching as well as his actions that mercy lies at the heart of kingdom values.[16] Perhaps one of the most well-known of all Bible stories is the story of the 'Good Samaritan' in Luke 10. Rather than be side-tracked by a theological debate on the requirements of the law, Jesus told a story demonstrating that mercy was to be given on the basis of need. It is this need which makes someone our neighbour, and so the rightful recipient of care, rather than any ethnic or religious grouping.

Interestingly, mercy has received very little attention from the disciplines of either philosophy or psychology, other than as an adjunct to either justice or forgiveness. It seems to me that in whichever context it is exercised, the step before both having and expressing mercy is genuine empathy, seeing from the perspective of the other. When we do that, and find echoes in our own lives, we will be much less likely to rush to judgement or to be hardened to the sufferings of others, as were those who brought the woman mentioned above to Jesus. All too often judgement triumphs over mercy instead of the other way round.[17] In an era where instant news and unfettered opinions on the internet mean verbal cruelty is distressingly common and cyberbullying has become a significant cause of mental distress (and sometimes even loss of life), and where the level, scale and coverage of suffering risks us developing compassion fatigue, mercy perhaps has never been more needed, both inside and outside the Christian community.

Reflection questions

- What does the word 'mercy' mean to you?
- Are there any occasions when you have received mercy?
- Are there times when you have been able to be merciful, or others where it has been challenging?

Rizpah: Protest

Rizpah daughter of Aiah took sackcloth and
spread it out for herself on a rock. From the be-
ginning of the harvest till the rain poured down
from the heavens on the bodies, she did not let
the birds touch them by day or the wild animals
by night.

2 Sam. 21:10

The voice of Rizpah

Not my boys. Not my beautiful boys. My heart is broken.

And I am angry.

Sometimes I question God. My life has never been straight-forward. First, I caught the eye of Saul, and entered that strange, half-life as his concubine, a wife yet not a wife. Then that awful time with Abner. Sometimes I have felt powerless and helpless. Not this time. Not when it comes to my sons.

There was nothing I could do to stop the soldiers coming. They took Armoni first – I could see the look of resignation in his eyes and all I could do was hope he could read the love in mine. I knew my sons would die with dignity, remembering that they were, after all, sons of the king. Then my Mephibosheth. I heard his namesake, the poor cripple, had been spared, and I hated myself for thinking for a moment that I wished it had been the other way around.

For a brief time I was simply numb. It was as though there was a gaping hole where my heart had once been, just empty space where all that fierce mother's love had resided. I was overwhelmed with grief and wanted my life to end, to join my sons in Sheol. But that feeling did not last for long. Instead, from deep within me rose a fury, a sense of terrible injustice that my family, what there was of it, should be sacrificed to supply restitution, whether to men or God. That anger grew even stronger, a volcano raging within me, when I heard that the bodies of my sons and the others had simply been left on the hillside, a demeaning end for my beloved and noble sons as though they were common criminals.

I could do nothing for them now except protect them in death, even though I was powerless to do so when they lived. So I set off for the hillside, setting my sackcloth of mourning down on the rock. I refused to let them be defiled. I lit a fire to keep the wolves away. When the birds came, I ran at them, beating them back, almost relieved to give vent to my wrath, to alleviate my helplessness by rushing in circles screaming at them, waving my sackcloth like a sword.

Day after day passed, then weeks, then months, the nights the longest and at times the most frightening, never knowing if I might be attacked by animals or men. Yet still I waited, still I defended the bodies which slowly changed, my boys becoming mere disfigured shadows of how I chose to remember them. The local village women sometimes brought food, from pity, or perhaps from relief it was not their sons lying there.

Sometimes I prayed, sometimes I railed against God, or the king. Sometimes I wept, until there were no tears left.

And then, I am told, word reached the king. I like to think my actions shamed him, though I will never know. I later discovered he went himself on the long journey to get the bones of my Saul and Jonathan. Others came to me, collecting the bones of my seven companions and taking them for burial. At last, they were given the dignity they deserved.

I had won. Now I could be at peace.

2 Samuel tells her story:

During the reign of David, there was a famine for three successive years; so David sought the face of the Lord. The Lord said, 'It is on account of Saul and his blood-stained house; it is because he put the Gibeonites to death.'

The king summoned the Gibeonites and spoke to them. (Now the Gibeonites were not a part of Israel but were survivors of the Amorites; the Israelites had sworn to spare them, but Saul in his zeal for Israel and Judah had tried to annihilate them.) David asked the Gibeonites, 'What shall I do for you? How shall I make atonement so that you will bless the Lord's inheritance?'

The Gibeonites answered him, 'We have no right to demand silver or gold from Saul or his family, nor do we have the right to put anyone in Israel to death.'

'What do you want me to do for you?' David asked.

They answered the king, 'As for the man who destroyed us and plotted against us so that we have been decimated and have no place anywhere in Israel, let seven of his male descendants be given to us to be killed and their bodies exposed before the Lord at Gibeah of Saul – the Lord's chosen one.'

So the king said, 'I will give them to you.'

The king spared Mephibosheth son of Jonathan, the son of Saul, because of the oath before the LORD between David and Jonathan son of Saul. But the king took Armoni and Mephibosheth, the two sons of Aiah's daughter Rizpah, whom she had borne to Saul, together with the five sons of Saul's daughter Merab, whom she had borne to Adriel son of Barzillai the Meholathite. He handed them over to the Gibeonites, who killed them and exposed their bodies on a hill before the LORD. All seven of them fell together; they were put to death during the first days of harvest, just as the barley harvest was beginning.

Rizpah daughter of Aiah took sackcloth and spread it out for herself on a rock. From the beginning of the harvest till the rain poured down from the heavens on the bodies, she did not let the birds touch them by day or the wild animals by night. When David was told what Aiah's daughter Rizpah, Saul's concubine, had done, he went and took the bones of Saul and his son Jonathan from the citizens of Jabesh Gilead. (They had stolen their bodies from the public square at Beth Shan, where the Philistines had hung them after they struck Saul down on Gilboa.) David brought the bones of Saul and his son Jonathan from there, and the bones of those who had been killed and exposed were gathered up.

They buried the bones of Saul and his son Jonathan in the tomb of Saul's father Kish, at Zela in Benjamin, and did everything the king commanded. After that, God answered prayer on behalf of the land.

(2 Sam. 21:1–14)

Exploration of protest

On 20 August 2018, aged just 15, Greta Thunberg began a solitary climate protest at the government buildings in

Stockholm. Since then, of course, she has become an international figure, addressing the COP25 gathering and sparking a number of other protests, bigger than her first. While she is not alone in beginning her protest individually, certainly solo protests are less usual than those by groups of varying sizes, though one may lead to the other. My 7-year-old grandson recently came home from school fascinated by the story of Rosa Parks, who in an initial solo protest refused to give up her seat on a racially segregated bus to a white person and was arrested as a result. Martin Luther King proposed a citywide boycott of public transport at a church meeting the next day, action which was eventually successful in ending segregation on public transport in Montgomery. He went on, of course, to become the dominant figure in the civil rights movement and was a strong believer that peaceful protest was the most effective weapon against societal injustice. He is perhaps best known for his 1963 speech 'I Have a Dream'[1] and his activism was underpinned by his faith.

Rizpah's protest, coming in the culturally very different biblical era, nevertheless shares some features with protests from across the ages. To begin with, most people's journey starts from a cause they feel strongly about, and it is that strength of feeling, their passion about the issue, which leads to the protest. Greta Thunberg began by hearing about climate change and not understanding why more was not being done.

Rizpah's protest is birthed in a situation which originated with King David asking God about a famine they were experiencing, and believing God told him that it was because of a wrong done to the Gibeonites. It was an era when if something went wrong, it was often assumed it was directly linked with God punishing an individual or a nation. Saul had agreed to leave the Gibeonites in peace but it seems he had reneged on that agreement and many of them had been killed. This was an era of bloodguilt, where bloodshed was common but there was still a moral code about murder. David asked them how this wrong could be rectified. They were working on an eye for an eye principle and demanded the death of seven of Saul's sons (seven signifying the number of completion). So David handed over to the Gibeonites the other two of Saul's sons, whose mother was his concubine Rizpah, and his five grandsons. All seven were killed.[2]

We would probably not see the link between sin, suffering and punishment this straightforwardly, believing in a more general view of the impact of sin in the world. That said, we can think in that way too at times when things go wrong, feeling, whatever our theology, that God is punishing us through difficult life circumstances. I've certainly had that said to me as a minister many times, but it is not that simple. Sometimes our actions have consequences, but often there is no easy explanation and I don't believe it is God punishing us.[3]

Rizpah's protest had its origins in both the pain and injustice of the death of her sons. Apart from the indescribably terrible loss of her two children, women in those days were entirely dependent on male relatives to provide for them financially. She was destitute. But it is more than just their death which leads to her actions. In those days to humiliate a family, you left a person unburied, as was done for example with criminals. Giving someone an honourable burial is so important – the last loving act you can do for them. She is being deprived even of that.

Rizpah could have just left it there, devastated but helpless. She had no power in any court. But no. She goes to the killing ground and refuses to leave. Her protest is both solo and silent. She could not prevent their deaths but she is determined to honour their humanity. Brutality would not have the last word. So she keeps vigil for all seven of them, not just her sons, from April till autumn. It is interesting that the protest which began from love for her sons became a wider protest, and though her primary motivation, as far as we can tell, was not an act of defiance to the king, she must have realised it was. Her protest is effective, and she does not just get justice and a proper burial for the seven she has protected, but also for Saul and Jonathan who – despite David's love for them – had not been treated with honour in death.

Researchers in the Netherlands found, in a fascinating study,[4] that although all protests are unique, there are five strands they hold in common. The first is a grievance, where anger is turned into action. Perhaps for Christians this might link with the practice of lament – something which is all too often underused. In some Christian churches, the emphasis in teaching and worship is on triumph. Good Friday is skipped over, sometimes not even part of the life of the church, in favour of Easter Sunday. Yet the Bible, in particular the Psalms but also elsewhere, gives space for lament, and grief and anger at injustice are closely linked. The second feature of protest is efficacy – the belief the protestor can change an outcome. Identity – identifying with the group or cause – is also important, and emotions are too, with anger the one most likely to lead to conflict with the authorities. The final one is social embeddedness – people coming together. We can see how recent protests, such as on climate change, Black Lives Matter, and the protests about the 2022 war in Ukraine are facilitated by the internet and social media allowing people to connect more easily.

Christian attitudes to protest have varied. There are certainly aspects of Jesus' life which either directly or indirectly challenge those in power and authority. He directly criticised

the Pharisees for hypocrisy. He modelled a very different attitude to women – they supported his ministry financially and
sat at his feet as disciples,[5] which usually was the province of
men with their rabbi. In the temple, outraged at its misuse, his
protest became physical, overturning tables and calling out the
wrongdoing.[6] Jesus never carried a placard, but we could argue
that his entire life was an act of protest. We rightly understand
the cross in terms of redemption, but is it not perhaps, in con-
junction with the resurrection, also the ultimate act of protest
against violence?

Despite the example of Jesus, Christians have found adopt-
ing the right attitude to protest complex. The first area which
can be problematic is choosing which issues to protest about.
The starting point for many, understandably, is the teaching
of the Bible, but this still does not necessarily prove straightforward. For example, some Christians have historically been
involved in protests in relation to the laws surrounding abor-
tion, yet this is a highly complex issue, beyond the scope of
this book, towards which Christians themselves have a range
of responses. Certainly some of the methods employed in such
protests, for example bombing clinics, are mercifully rare and
often perpetrated by lone individuals,[7] and seem to most of us
to be morally wrong as well as illegal. The recent involvement
of many Christians in protests against climate change comes
from the clear biblical mandate to care for creation, which on
the face of it is less divisive, yet even here a few would see this
world as in time being replaced by a new one and therefore see
less urgency in preserving it.

The next issue to wrestle with is what expressions of protest
are legitimate for Christians? People of faith often have particular concerns over the necessity for protests to be non-violent
and peaceful. More complex is the issue of civil disobedience

and the desire to reconcile protest with the command to 'be subject to the governing authorities, for there is no authority except that which God has established'.[8] At what point, if ever, does the significance and urgency of the issue we are addressing override that command? The disciples are forbidden by the authorities to speak about Jesus yet disobey the instruction, believing the demands of the gospel to be pre-eminent.[9]

There is an important missional question here – are Christians only known for what we are against? Can our protest instead be constructive, speaking primarily positively, calling for hope, justice and honesty in our national and international life?

Proverbs directs us to 'Speak up for those who cannot speak for themselves, for the rights of all who are destitute', to 'Speak up and judge fairly; defend the rights of the poor and needy'.[10] Both Rizpah's and Jesus' lives of protest originated in a sense of injustice which had its roots in love for others. Perhaps amid the complexity of our decision making, this is an important place to start and against which to measure our protests?

Reflection questions

- Have you ever been involved in any form of protest? Was it effective?
- What are the political or social issues which you feel strongly about?
- What kind of protest do you think Christians should, or should not, be involved with?

Solomon: Wisdom

Give me wisdom and knowledge, that I may lead this people, for who is able to govern this great people of yours?

2 Chr. 1:10

The voice of the woman

There is very little I have been proud of in my life. Like every child I had such hopes and dreams: security, and a family who loved me. But life threw me such bitter punches, and in the end there was nothing left for me but to sell the one last thing I possessed: myself. And there was always someone willing to pay.

I suppose it was inevitable. One month the blood did not come. Or the next. I felt different, as though my body was not quite my own. A mixture of terror and exhilaration grew within me. How would I manage to feed myself when my stomach swelled and my state was obvious? What right had I to bring a child into my shabby life? Would the women shun me and the men stone me? And yet . . . here at last there would be something good, something pure and lovely in my lonely life. Perhaps God still had something for me.

I met Talya one night as we both waited for trade in the shadows on the outskirts of the village. We shared secrets, as women do, and we found that we both had babies growing inside us, due in the month of Tishrei. It made me smile: a new year and perhaps a new start for us both. We decided to share a simple home together, to be there for one another as no one else would.

When my time came it was a struggle and I thought I would die. Talya held my hand and encouraged me, strengthening me. Just as I thought I could do no more, with one last exhausted push, there he was. She laid him on my breast and as he gazed at me, I thought my heart would burst. I named him Amram, after the father of Moses, Aaron and Miriam. Perhaps he too would grow to father people of greatness.

Three days later, it was Talya's turn, and mine to hold her as she cried out. She named him Rafael. Her angel.

Exhausted, I slept deeply for a time that night. Even before I opened my eyes, as sleep began to ebb away, I sensed something was wrong. The baby in my arms was cold and lifeless. I howled, a call of anguish into the early dawn. And then I stopped. And looked. This was not my Amram. It was Rafael. She must have rolled on him in the night and put him in my arms, taking Amram.

Bewildered and confused, I shrieked for Talya to come to me. I thought she was my friend. I was distraught for her, but how could she do this? She clasped Amram to her, denying what she had done. I tried to get her to admit it, said we would face her pain together, but she was adamant.

The village heard our shouting and, unsure what to do, took us to the king. I was so frightened. Solomon was terrifying and I dreaded his response. Perhaps he would punish us both. He told us to place the baby on a stool between us. Neither of us would give way, both claiming he was ours.

For a long time the king looked at us and at the baby, sitting in silence. The only sound I could hear was my heart pounding. When finally he spoke, to my horror it was to call for a sword to cut the baby, my Amram, in two. His servant held it aloft. I could not believe what I heard. I would not let my baby die. 'No, King,' I said. 'Give him to her.' Talya stood firm, and though at that moment I loathed her, I could hear the pain underneath the fury and hatred that spewed from her as she spat out the words: 'Yes. Let's neither of us have him.'

The king paused only for a moment and then, to my relief, to thanks I could not articulate, ordered that my Amram be returned to me.

I had heard he was wise, but now I have seen it for myself. I don't know what the future holds, but I have my Amram, and he is safe. For now, that is enough.

1 Kings tells part of this story:

Now two prostitutes came to the king and stood before him. One of them said, 'Pardon me, my lord. This woman and I live in the same house. I had a baby while she was there with me. The third day after my child was born, this woman also had a baby. We were alone; there was no one in the house but the two of us.

'During the night this woman's son died because she lay on him. So she got up in the middle of the night and took my son from my side while I your servant was asleep. She put him by her breast and put her dead son by my breast. The next morning, I got up to nurse my son – and he was dead! But when I looked at him closely in the morning light, I saw that it wasn't the son I had borne.'

The other woman said, 'No! The living one is my son; the dead one is yours.'

But the first one insisted, 'No! The dead one is yours; the living one is mine.' And so they argued before the king.

The king said, 'This one says, "My son is alive and your son is dead," while that one says, "No! Your son is dead and mine is alive."'

Then the king said, 'Bring me a sword.' So they brought a sword for the king. He then gave an order: 'Cut the living child in two and give half to one and half to the other.'

The woman whose son was alive was deeply moved out of love for her son and said to the king, 'Please, my lord, give her the living baby! Don't kill him!'

But the other said, 'Neither I nor you shall have him. Cut him in two!'

Then the king gave his ruling: 'Give the living baby to the first woman. Do not kill him; she is his mother.'

When all Israel heard the verdict the king had given, they held the king in awe, because they saw that he had wisdom from God to administer justice.

(1 Kgs 3:16–28)

Exploration of wisdom

Wisdom is a word we use in various contexts, yet it can easily be confused with other qualities with which it is linked but from which it is distinct. The first of these is knowledge, an accrual of facts and information. In the story from 1 Kings, the starting place for Solomon was to find out what was happening in the scenario in front of him: the claims and counter-claims. Knowledge is perhaps the easiest thing to acquire: in our era information is available (albeit with varied accuracy) at the click of a mouse. Experience is gained through time and the different things in which we participate that will add to our knowledge, and potentially give us additional insights against which to compare our information so far. I may, for example, know the theory about how a car engine works, having studied it in books. If I then watch an engine being dismantled and put back together, or serviced, that experience will add considerably to my knowledge. Part of the reason for this difference is that knowledge alone is not sufficient without understanding (finding what the facts mean and how they link together).

There are, of course, different types of wisdom and various contexts in which they may be used. Indeed, we may be wise in many situations but lack wisdom in some others, as we all possess blind spots. I can usually be wise pastorally but have very little practical wisdom, and so in those areas need to call on help from others. Indeed, part of wisdom is realising the limitations we have. To return to the engine example, I may have studied its workings, and watched someone working on it, but might still be wiser not to attempt to tackle it myself.

The topic of wisdom has been studied in recent decades by psychologists though no clear theory has emerged, not least because there is a lack of clarity regarding the balance between intellectual knowledge, environmental factors and more intuitive and emotional aspects, including personality. The existing theories tend to centre around outcomes, such as being able to solve personal dilemmas, advise others, or offer helpful involvement in society. Understandably, given the inability to have clarity on the exact components of wisdom, there are few empirical studies, with most research involving examining the writings of others. One of the most quoted researchers on wisdom is German psychologist Paul Baltes. He used five criteria to assess wisdom: factual knowledge (particularly about human nature), strategies for tackling issues, an understanding of social contexts and their change over time, being aware of cultural and value differences, and recognising that knowledge is limited and so there is a place for uncertainty. Although age is a factor, age alone does not equate to wisdom and it is, of course, possible to be older and not wise. In fact, research by Baltes and others suggests that wisdom does increase with age but is most present in middle-aged adults.[1] Although much research has centred on wisdom exhibited in problem solving and behaviour, some have sought to link it with other aspects such as creativity and curiosity.[2]

What is clear is that wisdom both involves reflecting on our knowledge, experience and understanding, and going a step beyond them. Psalm 119:130 says, 'The unfolding of your words gives light; it gives understanding to the simple.' We can read, even memorise, the Bible, but unless we gain understanding of it, through study and experience, we may struggle to wisely apply it to our lives. Biblically, that understanding also needs to be underpinned by our trust in God.[3]

For people of faith, wisdom has clear moral implications: it is 'pure; then peace-loving, considerate, submissive, full of mercy and good fruit, impartial and sincere',[4] and will be expressed by a 'good life, by deeds done in the humility that comes from wisdom'.[5] While our learning and life experiences may be an important part of gaining wisdom, true wisdom is God's gift. Solomon's wisdom is portrayed as exactly that. Earlier in 1 Kings 3 and also in 2 Chronicles 1 an account is given of God appearing to Solomon at night (1 Kings 3 specifies in a dream), and saying to Solomon that he will grant him anything he asks for. Solomon asks for 'wisdom and knowledge',[6] specifically in the account in 1 Kings 'a discerning heart to govern your people and to distinguish between right and wrong'.[7] God is pleased with his choice and so also gifts him 'wealth and honour' and, if he is obedient, long life.[8]

As well as us seeking to receive wisdom as an individual gift, there is also a strength in collective decision making, where each person or group of people can bring different components and perspectives. Paul prays for the church at Philippi that their love will 'abound more and more in knowledge and depth of insight, so that you may be able to discern what is best and may be pure and blameless for the day of Christ'.[9]

The Bible is a collection of books of different genres. These can vary slightly in the ways they are categorised, but one delineation includes historical (for example 1 Kings), law (such as Leviticus), poetry (Song of Songs would be in this group), prophecy (including both major prophets such as Isaiah and minor prophets such as Hosea), gospels (Matthew, Mark, Luke and John) and epistles or letters (such as 1 and 2 Corinthians). The remaining genre, relevant to our discussion here, is wisdom literature. Proverbs, Job and Ecclesiastes are part of this grouping in the Protestant Bible. The Roman Catholic Bible and that of the Eastern Churches (the Greek Orthodox church, for example) also include Ecclesiasticus and the Wisdom of Solomon. Within these books there are different kinds of wisdom writings. The first is sayings about a myriad of different life experiences. Some are short, succinct statements, often with examples taken from nature. A number of these are found in Proverbs, such as Proverbs 20:4: 'Sluggards do not plough in season; so at harvest time they look but find nothing.' This link with nature makes sense if God, as creator, has woven aspects of himself into the fabric of the universe, a thought which Paul takes up in Romans 1:20: 'For since the creation of the world God's invisible qualities – his eternal power and divine nature – have been clearly seen, being understood from what has been made'. Others are slightly longer sayings, with the same kind of general life wisdom.[10] A second group is wisdom from the royal courts, including those outlining correct behaviour: 'When you sit to dine with a ruler, note well what is before you, and put a knife to your throat if you are given to gluttony.'[11] A third kind is deeper reflection on some of the complex theological questions: the entire book of Job is an obvious example.

One of the features of wisdom literature is the personification of wisdom as female. She calls out, was there at creation, and encourages God's people to seek to live well.[12] In the New Testament, Jesus becomes the one who embodies wisdom. We have little information about Jesus' growing years, but we are told that 'he was filled with wisdom, and the grace of God was on him'.[13] Jesus' teaching led people to marvel at his wisdom.[14] Matthew in his gospel recognises the wisdom of Solomon, but asserts that Jesus is greater than him.[15] Paul puts it more strongly: 'Christ the power of God and the wisdom of God.'[16] Like the wisdom figure in Proverbs, 'He was with God in the beginning. Through him all things were made; without him nothing was made that has been made.'[17] The cross, which seemed at the time a foolish defeat, is in fact the way in which God subverts apparent wisdom and brings new life.[18] In relationship with him, as we grow increasingly to look like him, wisdom is ours both to ask for and to receive.[19]

Reflection questions

- What examples of wisdom have you seen in others?
- Can you think of any other examples of wisdom in the Bible apart from Solomon and Jesus?
- Are there any situations in your life at the moment where you need the wisdom God has promised?

Jezebel: Power

*As soon as Jezebel heard that Naboth had been
stoned to death, she said to Ahab, 'Get up and
take possession of the vineyard of Naboth the
Jezreelite that he refused to sell you. He is no
longer alive, but dead.'*

1 Kgs 21:15

The voice of Jezebel

No irrelevant peasant landowner was going to defeat me. Or
my husband, sullen and foolish though he could be so often.
No. Not me. I was the daughter of a king and now I am the
wife of one. What I say goes and I will tolerate no interference.

It was like this. I arrived home that day from surveying my
domain to find my husband in one of his moods. I'm no fool.
I know our marriage was more of a political alliance than anything else. I know too he is only king because his father was
and is not suited to the task. What do I care? Yes, it means I've
been sent to this pathetic little country with the tin-pot god
they all think is so special. As if their Yahweh could compare to
our Baal-Melkart. I make sure they worship my god and I get

rid of their foolish so-called prophets like squashing roaches in a grain store. I am queen and Ahab is no match for my feminine wiles. He does what I say and so does everyone else. I bend people to my will and if that fails, I just break them, like snapping a dry twig that's fallen in my path.

So, I knew that day I could rouse Ahab from his bed. Painting on a patient smile I asked him what was wrong. What a pitiful fool he is. It was all about the vineyard he had been whining to me about, daydreaming over it from the upper palace windows, wanting to use it to grow vegetables. It was nothing compared to the lush green beauty of my land, but no matter. He'd asked the owner to buy it, even offered him either a better one, or the money. Fools both – Ahab for offering to buy what he could just take, and this Naboth for refusing because it was some family plot.

It was no way for a king to behave. I told him to stop that nonsense and get up. Can't let the servants see him like that. I would do what I always did and sort it out. And I did. I wrote letters pretending to be my useless husband to the city rulers, the heads of the significant families, ordering them to proclaim a special occasion and give Naboth a place of honour. He was a person of influence in their community so no one would suspect a thing. Then, just as he was enjoying himself, two good-for-nothings I'd paid to do my bidding claimed he had blasphemed their god – might as well be useful for something – and the king. I know their ridiculous laws. It had to be that crime, so that this Naboth could be stoned to death and Ahab could legitimately take over the land. His family would lose their land and be thrown on the street but I cared nothing for that. Problem solved, vineyard Ahab's. Easy.

The story was not quite over, admittedly. That troublesome so-called prophet Elijah came and sought Ahab out. Threatened him, no less! As if he or his god have the power to wipe any of us out.

He can say what he likes. I am Jezebel, and no one is going to defeat me.

1 Kings tells part of her story:

Some time later there was an incident involving a vineyard belonging to Naboth the Jezreelite. The vineyard was in Jezreel, close to the palace of Ahab king of Samaria. Ahab said to Naboth, 'Let me have your vineyard to use for a vegetable garden, since it is close to my palace. In exchange I will give you a better vineyard or, if you prefer, I will pay you whatever it is worth.'

But Naboth replied, 'The LORD forbid that I should give you the inheritance of my ancestors.'

So Ahab went home, sullen and angry because Naboth the Jezreelite had said, 'I will not give you the inheritance of my ancestors.' He lay on his bed sulking and refused to eat.

His wife Jezebel came in and asked him, 'Why are you so sullen? Why won't you eat?'

He answered her, 'Because I said to Naboth the Jezreelite, "Sell me your vineyard; or if you prefer, I will give you another vineyard in its place." But he said, "I will not give you my vineyard."'

Jezebel his wife said, 'Is this how you act as king over Israel? Get up and eat! Cheer up. I'll get you the vineyard of Naboth the Jezreelite.'

So she wrote letters in Ahab's name, placed his seal on them, and sent them to the elders and nobles who lived in Naboth's city with him. In those letters she wrote:

'Proclaim a day of fasting and give Naboth a prominent seat among the people. But put two scoundrels opposite him and get them to bring charges that he has cursed both God and the king. Then take him out and stone him to death.'

So the elders and nobles who lived in Naboth's city did as Jezebel directed in the letters she had written to them. They proclaimed a fast and seated Naboth in a prominent place among the people. Then two scoundrels came and sat opposite him and brought charges against Naboth before the people, saying, 'Naboth has cursed both God and the king.' So they took him outside the city and stoned him to death. Then they sent word to Jezebel: 'Naboth has been stoned to death.'

As soon as Jezebel heard that Naboth had been stoned to death, she said to Ahab, 'Get up and take possession of the vineyard of Naboth the Jezreelite that he refused to sell you. He is no longer alive, but dead.' When Ahab heard that Naboth was dead, he got up and went down to take possession of Naboth's vineyard.

Then the word of the LORD came to Elijah the Tishbite: 'Go down to meet Ahab king of Israel, who rules in Samaria. He is now in Naboth's vineyard, where he has gone to take possession of it. Say to him, "This is what the LORD says: have you not murdered a man and seized his property?" Then say to him, "This is what the Lord says: in the place where dogs licked up Naboth's blood, dogs will lick up your blood – yes, yours!"'

Ahab said to Elijah, 'So you have found me, my enemy!'

'I have found you,' he answered, 'because you have sold yourself to do evil in the eyes of the LORD. He says, "I am going to bring disaster on you. I will wipe out your descendants and cut off from Ahab every last male in Israel – slave or free. I will make your house like that of Jeroboam son of Nebat and that of Baasha son of Ahijah, because you have aroused my anger and have caused Israel to sin."

'And also concerning Jezebel the LORD says: "Dogs will devour Jezebel by the wall of Jezreel."

'Dogs will eat those belonging to Ahab who die in the city, and the birds will feed on those who die in the country.'

(1 Kgs 21:1–24)

Exploration of power

I doubt if anyone would ever name their child 'Jezebel'. She has come to epitomise the personification of an evil woman and her name is used in literature and song in the same derogatory way. Perhaps, however, there is rather more to her. For centuries the Bible was read through particular eyes, inevitably impacted by the cultural assumptions of what women were expected to be. Some theologians such as Phyllis Trible have more recently sought in various ways to take a fresh look at biblical women, though such authors too, as all of us, will bring their own cultural context, personal story and assumptions to the task. That said, it can be difficult to see a different, more sympathetic side to Jezebel. She eclipses even Delilah and Potiphar's wife, who both misuse their sexuality. Unlike them, she is an unashamed murderess.

It is important nonetheless to recognise that, as always, there was a backstory. Undoubtedly her marriage would have been primarily a political one motivated by trade routes and military protection. The biblical account tells us nothing of how she felt about this, and to be sent from her homeland to the very different geographical and cultural context of Israel must have been difficult. She does show a certain determination and strength of character in keeping to her own religion rather than simply being subsumed by that of her new husband: though, of course, this paganism was exactly what the biblical writers wanted to condemn. Is the frightening woman she becomes a reaction to the extreme change in her circumstance, combined with Ahab's apparent weakness? And was her dressing herself in finery and make-up at the end of her life seeking to misuse her sexuality to save herself by entrapping Jehu, or in fact facing what she knew was inevitable with what a friend of mine once referred to, in a time of difficulty, as 'warpaint'?[1]

We can never be sure of her motivation, but it is clear that Jezebel was a woman of power. There are many different kinds of power, and they are exercised in different ways, both formally and personally. In 1959, social psychologists John R.P. French and Bertram Raven identified five types of power, with a sixth added in 1965.[2] Formal power, they asserted, comes in at least three types. The first is coercive: a form of power linked with the ability of the person to punish anyone who is non-compliant. There were certainly elements of this kind of power wielded by Jezebel, as there are also, regrettably, in some working situations where, for example, the threat of redundancy is used as a means of control. The second form is reward power, where rewards, either verbal or tangible, are used to obtain what is wanted. The next is legitimate power, which exists because of the person's position within a group or organisation: heads of armed services, or political regimes would be examples and certainly for Jezebel, her position as queen was an element in the power she wielded. At a more personal level, people may find power in their expertise, particularly if it is unusual or needed in a situation of crisis. The medical experts arguably had additional power during the Covid pandemic. There is referent power: this is the ability of a person to wield power because they are respected or admired. The final type of power, which was the one French and Raven added later, is informational power, which is based on the person's ability to control the flow of information: a form of power seen in some tyrannies. Different types of power may, of course, be more or less effective depending on the context: a national emergency calls for resources different from those appropriate for a personal or work relationship.

Joseph Nye, the American political scientist, has suggested a different way of looking at power, described as 'hard' power and 'soft' power. Hard power is the kind often seen in international settings and traditionally assumed to be the most effective: force or the threat of force, economic sanctions and the kinds of coercion achieved by military or economic might. The war in Ukraine, which began on 24 February 2022, has seen these kinds of power exercised by the various nations involved. In contrast, Nye argues, soft power seeks cooperation through persuasion, such as the use of international rules and good communication between groups and nations.

One of the frustrations ordinary people have towards those who hold, for example, political power, is their capacity to not live up to the behaviour which might be expected of those in high office, whether demonstrated by moral lapses or financial impropriety. Psychologists refer to this as the paradox of power: many people gain power through having qualities which are attractive, yet when in power these very aspects take on a darker hue – assertiveness becomes bullying, for example. A colleague of mine regularly said that our greatest strengths can become our greatest weaknesses. This tendency to lack self-awareness was one of the reasons that in former times the court jesters were so useful, having the rare capacity to puncture the self-importance of rulers.[3]

While people sometimes obtain power because they are respected and liked, once in power the position they hold can make them less sympathetic to the concerns of others, a second cry of despair often railed against politicians. This suspicion is, however, more than anecdotal: the psychologist Adam

Galinsky conducted studies which suggested that people in positions of power find it easier to rationalise their lapses. For example, they believe that they can break speed limits, unlike others, because they are important people who need to get to their next appointment.[4] These changes are then exacerbated if the person in power is treated differently, for example with great deference, by those around them. This potential diminishing of empathy in people who obtain power has been discussed in various settings.[5]

Another possible difficulty in holding power is that sometimes those in power can overestimate the likelihood of success and underestimate the risks. The disastrous sinking of the *Titanic*, for example, was in part because the ship was considered to be unsinkable and because the warnings of icebergs were ignored.

It is difficult to know what babies feel or think, but many psychologists and psychoanalysts assume that at the start of life babies feel very powerful – they cry, and someone comes, at least with a reasonably good caregiver. As we grow to the toddler stage, we realise that it is a big world and we do not control it, which is so terrifying we seek to take control, or power, where we can, and temper tantrums are one result when this wish to control is frustrated. This continues in adulthood as we discover more about our mortality and the capacity of random events to disrupt our lives. The way that we respond to people in positions of power in adulthood will be influenced by these various previous experiences, including of our parents, who in our early years hold enormous power over us, and also other authority figures, such as teachers. In the process psychologists refer to as transference, we treat people in power and authority 'as if' they were those we have experienced before.[6] Our attitudes to those in power are therefore impacted by our internal world as well as the actual behaviour of those in power.

Power, however, is not only or necessarily negative; indeed, in itself it is neutral. It is what it is used for, and the impact on the well-being of any people affected by its use, which gives it moral value. It can be a resource, something which enables good. It may also be not just the power to make something happen, but also the power *not* to do something, the use of restraint or self-control for our benefit or that of others.

Biblically, power is associated first and foremost with God, and because God is personal, that power is not seen as a force, as was the case in Greek thinking, but a part of God's nature, along with other qualities, such as love and mercy. This power is seen first in creation; as quoted previously, Paul wrote that 'since the creation of the world God's invisible qualities – his eternal power and divine nature – have been clearly seen'.[7] The prophet Jeremiah records God saying that 'with my great power and outstretched arm I made the earth and its people and the animals that are on it'.[8] Many would say that in a storm there is a sense of the immense power in creation and Job, after all his questioning, experiences God's response in the same way.[9] The Old Testament writers saw God's power used at times to protect his people, such as in the account of the Exodus, and at other times given to people to enable them to fulfil his purposes. When needed God also 'gives strength to the weary and increases the power of the weak'.[10]

In the New Testament, the birth of Jesus is made possible as the Holy Spirit comes upon Mary and 'the power of the Most High' overshadows her.[11] The power of God is demonstrated through Jesus' control over nature, sickness and demons.[12] Most supremely it was demonstrated in the resurrection: 'That power is the same as the mighty strength he exerted when he raised Christ from the dead and seated him at his right hand in the heavenly realms'.[13] For Paul, the gospel was 'the power of God',[14] releasing Christians from the grip of sin in their lives and giving the means to live as God intends through the Spirit of God living within, and growing the fruit of 'love, joy, peace, forbearance, kindness, goodness, faithfulness, gentleness and self-control'.[15] It was a power which, as we will see in Chapter 20, was often most evident in Paul's own weakness. At times this was in his preaching: 'My message and my preaching were not with wise and persuasive words, but with a demonstration of the Spirit's power'.[16] At others it was seen in God's capacity to sustain him through personal difficulty, when Paul discovered, as others have across the centuries, that God's 'power is made perfect in weakness'.[17]

A very different kind of power.

Reflection questions

- What different kinds of power have you seen in different contexts – locally, nationally and internationally?
- In what ways can power be used for good?
- How does the power of God differ from the power you have seen?

Jonah: Prejudice

But to Jonah this seemed very wrong, and he became angry.

Jonah 4:1

The voice of Jonah

I am so angry. At moments my whole body shakes with it, like a white light skulking behind my eyes, blinding me to everyone and everything else. At other times it is as if a cold mist descends, even in the heat of the day, and I'm overwhelmed by an energy-sapping indifference towards my life, my so-called calling and even you, God. And that is where my deepest fury is directed. At you.

You have blighted my life from the start. I did not ask to be called to speak out for you. That was your choice, not mine. When it was to your people, my people, it was tolerable, sometimes even a privilege. We are special, called by you, set apart. I was, and am, proud to be a Hebrew. It made me feel significant.

But then you told me to go to Nineveh.

Nineveh. Everything you hate, surely? The stories of the most appalling barbarity, unspeakable acts, that filter through to us from across the miles. At first, I thought I must have mis-heard you. Why would you speak to them? Yes, it was a warn-ing of destruction, but why would you want to alert them? Why not just destroy them as your enemies, our enemies? But your insistent voice, giving me no peace, would not let me ig-nore what you were saying.

So yes, I ran. What did you expect? That I would go will-ingly towards my possible destruction? I did not deserve to be torn to pieces for being faithful to you. And still you would not let me go. I was ready to die in that storm. Why didn't you let me? No, even then you had not finished with my torment. Instead, I found myself filthy, stinking of fish guts, on the shore. You had left me no choice. I set off into another, invisi-ble and internal, storm with the message you gave me. I yelled it out, making my way towards the centre of the city, my only consolation that I could at least briefly relish my proclamation of judgement. I was expecting at any moment to be hauled in front of the king, or simply dismembered by the hostile crowd. But no. To my shock, everywhere I went people listened. It was as if they already knew, that I had somehow spoken this simple message into ears and hearts which were prepared like farm-ing soil for planting. The king ordered corporate repentance and suddenly the whole city was fasting and wearing sackcloth. Even the animals! I was sickened.

I left the city and found refuge. For a time, I waited, think-ing you might still strike them down. As the time went by, I began to realise you were not going to. These wicked people were saying sorry and you were just letting them off the hook. I could not believe it. Not them, surely not them? Isn't it just us, your special people, that you show mercy to?

My waiting became bearable for a time with the plant. A small sign of something different, a little patch of green amid the grey outlook of the city. It was my companion for a season, something that did not judge me, that demanded nothing, that just let me be. Sheltered me from the burning, blinding sun. But then you destroyed that too.

So yes, I am angry beyond words. It's not fair. I've done what you said. I'm left looking a fool in this blistering heat while these evil pagans get your mercy. Aren't you supposed to treat us, your people, better than the rest? What happened to your special favour? What is the point if you can spare these foul brutes?

Amid my fury I hear your voice, insistent again, questioning me: why shouldn't you show them mercy? Right now, God, I'm too angry to answer, and I'm not sure, if my rage ever wanes, what my reply will be.

The book of Jonah tells part of his story:

But to Jonah this seemed very wrong, and he became angry. He prayed to the LORD, 'Isn't this what I said, LORD, when I was still at home? That is what I tried to forestall by fleeing to Tarshish. I knew that you are a gracious and compassionate God, slow to anger and abounding in love, a God who relents from sending calamity. Now, LORD, take away my life, for it is better for me to die than to live.'

But the LORD replied, 'Is it right for you to be angry?'

Jonah had gone out and sat down at a place east of the city. There he made himself a shelter, sat in its shade and waited to see what would happen to the city. Then the LORD God provided a leafy plant and made it grow up over Jonah to give shade for his head to ease his discomfort, and Jonah was very happy about the plant. But at dawn the next day God provided a worm, which chewed the plant so that it withered. When the sun rose, God provided a scorching east wind, and the sun blazed on Jonah's head so that he grew faint. He wanted to die, and said, 'It would be better for me to die than to live.'

But God said to Jonah, 'Is it right for you to be angry about the plant?'

'It is,' he said. 'And I'm so angry I wish I were dead.'

But the LORD said, 'You have been concerned about this plant, though you did not tend it or make it grow. It sprang up overnight and died overnight. And should I not have concern for the great city of Nineveh, in which there are more than a hundred and twenty thousand people who cannot tell their right hand from their left – and also many animals?'

(Jonah 4)

Exploration of prejudice

It is quite easy, isn't it, to sit rather loftily on our own high ground and pass judgement on Jonah? He is not the most likeable of biblical characters. Rebellious, sulky and selfish – in our honest moments, however, perhaps we can recognise that the reason we find Jonah such an unattractive personality is because we have those same qualities lurking inside us.

So, what is going on in this story? What can it teach us about our own attitudes?

Part of the difficulty in approaching this part of the Bible is that at least some of us have memories of it from childhood books, humorous cartoon pictures of a big fish being often the most prominent image. Yet for Jewish people, this story is both an important and a serious one. Every year on Yom Kippur – the Day of Atonement – Jonah is read across the world as part of a day which involves both corporate repentance and remembering who they are as the people of God. Various reasons are given for this reading, including as a reminder of God's mercy, his sovereignty over creation, the place of prayer and reiterating that as God's people they are called to be a blessing to the nations.[1] Whatever the variety of reasons, the reading of the book of Jonah being part of such a solemn and significant day is a warning to us not to consign it to the place of a humorous childhood story.

There are various opinions as to whether the book of Jonah is an allegory (where spiritual meaning is found in each detail), a parable (where the story as a whole brings the significance rather than the detail) or a historically accurate account. For our purposes, it does not matter which. Its importance comes in its salutary lesson that erroneous attitudes to others can be hiding within us, sometimes deeply buried and at other times much nearer the surface.

What was it that caused Jonah to so flagrantly disobey God, literally heading in the opposite direction, and to then behave like a sulking teenager when his mission was successful and the city was spared? Nineveh was the capital of the Assyrian Empire, which largely corresponded to what we now know as Iraq: it was situated on the Tigris River near what is now the city of Mosul. As a nation, Assyria was profoundly hostile to Israel. For Nineveh to be destroyed would undoubtedly have seemed to Jonah a vindication for his own people. It was an environment where evil flourished. They worshipped (ironically) both a fish god, Dagon, and the war god Ishtar and were ruthless in their attitude to peoples they conquered, plundering their cities and leading the people away, hooks in their noses like animals. Jonah had good reason to both fear and despise the people of Nineveh.

In contrast, we can infer the pride that Jonah takes in his own heritage, expressed in his words to the sailors: 'I am a Hebrew and I worship the LORD, the God of heaven, who made the sea and the dry land.'[2] Jonah, understandably though mistakenly, sees his own people as worthy of the compassion of God, but not the Ninevites, hence he chastises God: 'I knew that you are a gracious and compassionate God, slow to anger and abounding in love, a God who relents from sending calamity.'[3] He is able to feel compassion for the plant, in addition to the selfish motive that his shelter had been lost, but has none for the 'hundred and twenty thousand people who cannot tell their right hand from their left'.[4] We are left not knowing how Jonah responded, which leaves the way open for us to reflect on that question for ourselves. Which group of people, or even individual, would we be happier to see receive judgement than mercy?

There are many other lessons that can be drawn from this small but significant book, but for the purposes of this chapter, let's take a closer look at the way we too can be affected in our view of others – to begin to consider whether we may also be harbouring prejudice.

It may be helpful before we begin, to clarify some of the language used in this complex and difficult area. Prejudice refers to a view or feeling towards something or someone which has been formed prematurely or without proper evidence. It is, simply, pre-judging; determining our attitude to an issue, person or group of people without sufficient information. This attitude may be purely an intellectual belief, or may have feelings (such as like or dislike) attached. This affective, or emotional, component can include a wide range of very strong emotions. These attitudes may be caused in part by stereotyping. This word 'stereotype' originated with Firmin Didot (1764–1836), from printing: it was a kind of duplicate impression used for printing instead of the original. Stereotypes are particularly common in literature and drama: the troubled policeman, or the peculiar and immoral vicar (one of my pet hates – I do not know any ministers like that!). During the Covid pandemic, many church meetings went online. One social media post commented on how this change would be difficult for older people (in itself a vague grouping) because they were not computer literate or confident. This was in the most part completely untrue, with almost all older people, certainly in the church I was in, adapting easily to Zoom and livestreaming. Misinformation and generalising of this kind has the potential to lead on to discrimination, which moves beyond what we feel internally to actually treating someone or a group in a different way.

So put simply, stereotypes are set ideas or beliefs, prejudice is the resulting attitude, and discrimination describes resulting changes in behaviour – though this is not inevitable, and there can be prejudice which does not result in actions but remains internal. Prejudice articulated verbally is particularly problematic, with a delicate balancing act between free speech and unacceptable, damaging verbal communications which could, in the worst-case scenario, incite violence. Discrimination can be in many forms, including reduced access to services, biased portrayal in the media, differences in salary or recruitment, verbal insults, or in the worst instances, hate crime or even genocide. It can be practised by individuals, groups or institutions. Often the word 'discrimination' is used in situations where the treatment of an individual or group is less favourable, but it is not necessarily so, as for example in the use of positive discrimination in recruitment. This might be informal preferential attitudes or treatment, or more formalised procedures designed to compensate for inequalities which might otherwise exist. There are legal frameworks that are in place to minimise discrimination: in the UK, these include the Race Relations Act, the Sex Discrimination Act, and the Disability Discrimination Act.

How do our prejudices form? We are not told in the story of Jonah if he had any direct experiences of Ninevites, had heard stories, or if his attitude sprung from a more general view of any non-Israelite. Our experiences, particularly early ones, can create the seeds from which prejudice can grow. If we meet someone from a particular grouping who treats us badly, this can generalise in our thinking: one difficult relationship or experience of betrayal becomes 'men/women are not to be trusted', for example. Once a view is formed, it can be difficult to see other perspectives due to 'confirmation bias' – we tend to more readily pay attention to experiences which confirm our views. The experiences and impressions which lie at the root of our attitudes, if they are unconscious memories, can be particularly difficult to both uncover and subvert. In one sense, there is a parallel in the psychological process of transference mentioned previously, where we feel towards, or treat, someone differently because it is 'as if' they are another person. I once found myself treating a very new member of staff as if I had known him for years, only realising later that in one small physical aspect he reminded me of my father – a kind of positive stereotype. Transference can be triggered by a small feature in the person or situation and is an unconscious process which is explored in some forms of counselling and therapy.[5]

Not all of our prejudices originate with our own experiences, however. Children pick up impressions and views from many sources: parents, friends, teachers and the media – particularly, in older children, from social media. Most children and young people will absorb and adopt the social norms of the groups they find themselves in, particularly if it facilitates becoming accepted by that group. Later they may question these attitudes, but they can be very difficult to shift.

It is possible that some personality types, particularly authoritarian personalities, may be more prone to develop prejudicial attitudes.[6] This particular personality type can display a submissive attitude to authority figures, a rigidly hierarchical view of the world and a hostile attitude to those not of their own grouping. If this is the case, such a personality growing up in an environment where strong prejudices are the norm would be particularly susceptible to developing those views.

Studies in the past have suggested that prejudice can emerge between groups when resources are limited. In a classic study called 'The Robbers' Cave Study',[7] two groups of 11-year-old boys were sent to a remote summer camp. The groups named themselves and were involved in various tasks and competitions. Prejudice began to develop between the two groups, and was only minimised when the groups were made to work together towards common goals.

Another way of seeking to understand how prejudices develop is social identity theory. We all tend to naturally group things. This is seen even in children's play. For example, both our grandchildren at different stages have arranged cars by colour or trains by size. We categorise people in the same way, and often the groups we belong to, such as supporters of a particular football team, are a source of identity, self-esteem and pride. We are then prone to exaggerate the differences between groups, and the similarity within them, forming an in-group (the one to which we belong) and an out-group (others), bolstering our own esteem as belonging to the in-group. So, put simply, we categorise ourselves and others into a group, we identify with that group and its norms, and then we engage in comparison, needing to believe our group is the best. This seems at least partially to be true for Jonah. All of us are in different kinds of groups: such as those governed by our gender, nationality, race/ethnicity, social class, religion, age, sexual orientation, or profession. To varying degrees these will form a significant part of our identity and we need to guard against negative or stereotypical views of those in other groups.

Christianity is not immune from areas of stereotyping, prejudice or discrimination, indeed American psychologist Gordon Allport maintained Christians were less tolerant than other groups.[8] Like Jonah, Christians can see themselves as chosen and others as lesser. We too easily take the self-righteous stance of the elder brother rather than remember that we are all prodigals.[9] As a woman minister, I know some churches, when I looked to make a move, dismissed me as a possible next minister on the basis of my gender. Most of the attitudes I have experienced over the years are amusing – just yesterday I was conducting a funeral and, as we arrived early, the staff addressed my husband, assuming it must be him who was taking the service. Occasionally the attitudes are patronising – such as a meeting I attended as, at the time, the minister of a large church, where the gentleman sitting next to me patted me on the knee and said, 'Well, my dear . . .' At times they have been profoundly hurtful, though I am aware my experiences are mild compared to the horrific treatment of some of my female colleagues. More difficult to respond to are comments such as, 'I don't approve of women ministers, but you are alright.' While I hope to have at least subverted the prejudice displayed, the comment suggests the basic attitude remains unchanged – I am simply an anomaly. Some people who hold such views, of course, have thought them through carefully, based upon differences of theology and biblical interpretation, for which I have respect. Some, however, are clearly not, such as when I was told that all women's voices do not 'work' for preaching. Churches have displayed sickening racial prejudice at times – the first church I served in had Afro-Caribbean members who had in the past been shunned in other churches. Undoubtedly in more subtle forms prejudice and discrimination still exist, and it is important to see prejudice as a sin, in direct opposition to the generous and undiscriminating love of God.

More positively, the Christian community has the capacity to be a place where barriers are overcome. Jesus was radical in breaking down many social norms which divided people: he called outcasts to follow him, women provided for his ministry, and Mary sat at his feet in the way that usually only male disciples sat at the feet of rabbis.[10] Jesus commended non-Jews for their faith[11] and discussed theology with a Samaritan woman,[12] as we will see in a later chapter. As the early church began to find non-Jews among its members, Peter learned that 'God does not show favouritism'.[13] Paul, who had once had a deep prejudice towards followers of Jesus before encountering Jesus on the road to Damascus, came to see that 'There is neither Jew nor Gentile, neither slave nor free, nor is there male and female, for you are all one in Christ Jesus.'[14] As Christians of different genders, ethnic groups etc. worship and work together, prejudices can be eroded, as long as they are not simply relocated outside the group – 'all non-Christians are . . .' – or emerge in more subtle ways, such as excluding some from conversations in after-church coffee, or not inviting them to house groups or other church activities. The church in the UK has responded well to the war in the Ukraine, organising aid and welcoming refugees, but the challenge remains to reach out in the same way to every ethnic group, not only those who are similar to us. Good theology and teaching is key, with an emphasis, for example, on the universality of God's love and the work of

Christ. In our church practices we need to aim to have genuine inclusivity and try to be aware of the subtle ways in which people can be left out. In that way, churches have the potential to be much-needed places of genuine sanctuary and healing.

Reflection questions

- What attitudes to people who were different did you encounter when you were growing up?
- Have you ever been aware of prejudice in yourself towards others, or in others towards you?
- How inclusive are any groups in which you are involved?

11

Mary: Courage

'I am the Lord's servant,' Mary answered. 'May your word to me be fulfilled.'

Luke 1:38

The voice of Mary

Joseph has just left. The conversation didn't go well, but I did not really expect that it would. I can't blame him, or expect him to understand. I still can't grasp it myself.

I'm just an ordinary girl. My life was so neatly planned. Joseph and I were betrothed, it was all settled. A good man, an honest tradesman. He would look after me. My future lay with him, in Nazareth. I would bear his children and live out an unremarkable but contented life. He would take our children to the synagogue and I would teach them about Pesach and Shabbat, the special words and foods. I would fetch water with the other women and squeeze oil for cooking and, if God so blessed us, also to sell. I had lain awake at night thinking of how it would be. Yet nothing I had ever imagined came close to this.

The first question he asked me was how I knew it was an angel and not some strange dream as I dozed in the midday sun. I didn't know how to answer him. I just knew, though it took time to fully realise. He looked ordinary enough, yet there was something about him, an otherworldliness that somehow shone through even his everyday appearance. He had startled me, arriving as if from nowhere as I was sweeping out the small room where the animals slept. His greeting was hardly what I expected, either: 'Grace to you, who have found grace.'[1] I was alarmed as well as startled. Who started a conversation like that? What was this man doing, flaunting our customs by addressing me, a woman, with no one else there?

That was nothing compared to what came next. He spoke – as I began reeling with shock and fright – saying that I was to have a son, who he even named: Jesus, Rescuer. No ordinary child, though, Son of the Most High, David's descendent, the Messiah we have prayed for, longed for, waited for, generation after generation. I had prayed for him to come, like everyone else, but that I was to be a part of that plan – that, of course, was something I had never imagined. I could not work out what I felt: honoured, privileged, or simply terrified? Not only that, but it was impossible. I was not yet married to Joseph, so how could I have a child? I heard but could not fully understand what he was saying; that somehow this would be God's child, his creation in an even fuller sense than usual. And, as if to reassure me, as if comfort were even remotely possible, he told me that Elizabeth, my dear Elizabeth, who has known such heartache, is to have a child! Momentarily I forgot my own extraordinary news, with all its ramifications, for an amazed delight that Elizabeth was to receive what she so long had longed for and had given up hope of ever receiving. I turned back to try to absorb what my visitor was saying, as the repercussions swept over me. How could I explain this? What would those who loved me think of me, never mind those who didn't? And

Joseph. How could I tell him, smashing the dreams we shared? My heart was racing, and my mind too.

Yet, if this indeed was a messenger from Yahweh, who was I to argue? He had been faithful in the past and I must trust him for the future. So, quietly, hesitantly I said in reply: 'I am God's, all of me, and here to do his will.'

But now I sit here, the memory of Joseph's face, bewildered and hurt, vivid in my mind as my tears fall. Perhaps Joseph needs to see an angel too. Until he does, I can only wait, trust and pray.

Luke 1 tells part of her story:

In the sixth month of Elizabeth's pregnancy, God sent the angel Gabriel to Nazareth, a town in Galilee, to a virgin pledged to be married to a man named Joseph, a descendant of David. The virgin's name was Mary. The angel went to her and said, 'Greetings, you who are highly favoured! The Lord is with you.'

Mary was greatly troubled at his words and wondered what kind of greeting this might be. But the angel said to her, 'Do not be afraid, Mary, you have found favour with God. You will conceive and give birth to a son, and you are to call him Jesus. He will be great and will be called the Son of the Most High. The Lord God will give him the throne of his father David, and he will reign over Jacob's descendants for ever; his kingdom will never end.'

'How will this be,' Mary asked the angel, 'since I am a virgin?'

The angel answered, 'The Holy Spirit will come on you, and the power of the Most High will overshadow you. So the holy one to be born will be called the Son of God. Even Elizabeth your relative is going to have a child in her old age, and she who was said to be unable to conceive is in her sixth month. For no word from God will ever fail.'

'I am the Lord's servant,' Mary answered. 'May your word to me be fulfilled.' Then the angel left her.

(Luke 1:26–38)

Exploration of courage

We need to start our reflection on courage with a very important distinction. Courage is not about a lack of fear. If we feel no fear in a situation, for whatever reason, we do not need to be courageous. We display bravery when the fear is present, and real, but we still make the choice to take the action for which the courage is required. Indeed, the greater the fear, the more courage is required. I still feel nervous when I need to lead an important meeting, and need to galvanise myself to do so. However, if faced with a burning building where someone is shouting for help, it would be a completely different situation. Mary, in her remarkable acceptance of the unique role which she had been given, would undoubtedly have experienced fear at a number of levels and of several different kinds. Physically, she was probably still young and the prospect of a pregnancy and all it would entail, always risky without the modern facilities we now have in many countries, must have been daunting. How would she tell Joseph, her family and friends, and how would they respond? Her social contacts would be scandalised – who would support her, if anyone, and who would reject her? Emotionally, how could she process the overwhelming range of emotions from which she must have been reeling, both at this moment of announcement and, in reality, throughout her life? For Mary, physical, social and emotional courage were all needed to take on this extraordinary task.

There are many inspiring instances of these different kinds of courage being demonstrated by other individuals. Witold Pilecki was a Polish resistance leader, who among other things allowed himself to be captured and taken to Auschwitz, where he organised a resistance movement and had reports of the atrocities that were happening smuggled out. On a daily basis, members of the various emergency services demonstrate courage in the face of physical risks. Rosa Parks, mentioned earlier in this book, demonstrated courage in speaking out despite the social conditions of her day, and many social activists need similar courage. There are countless individuals requiring immense emotional courage as they face difficult family situations, diagnoses of terminal illness, or the challenges of living with mental health issues. Some instances of courage are in the moment, requiring a split-second decision, some are lived out over time, sometimes over years, giving the opportunity to weigh up options and continually count the cost. For Mary, there must have been both: if we do not have the whole conversation recorded in Luke's account, perhaps she had a little time to weigh things up, but ultimately her answer was in the moment. However, there must have been many times throughout her life when she needed courage as the mother of Jesus. One of the most profound examples must surely have been at Golgotha, where she stayed at the foot of the cross, enduring the most excruciating emotional pain of watching her son die in the most painful and humiliating of ways. The long-term endurance of suffering, of whatever kind, is courage of the highest calibre. We need to recognise the enormous toll that facing such situations with courage takes, often for the sake of family members and friends, and offer both support and safe spaces for the person to speak honestly about the cost for them.

The courage to choose to make major changes is another, sometimes unrecognised, form of bravery. It may be internal changes. In the counselling service I used to run, we once had a client who came for counselling for the first time in her nineties, recognising that there were aspects of her thinking and how she felt about herself and her life that needed to be addressed. It took a great deal of bravery.

The reason for, and type of, risk is important when we seek to assess courage. It is not the same, for example, as recklessness. To drive a motorbike at ninety miles an hour without a crash helmet is not courageous but foolhardy. We would not view as equally meritorious displaying courage in robbing a bank compared with diving into a river to save someone who is drowning. We would, quite naturally, have respect only for the latter.

It would seem that connection makes us more likely to display courageous behaviour. To return to the previous example, we might be more likely to dive in the river for someone we know, especially for someone we cared about, choosing instead to ring for help if the person was a stranger. That said, there are many instances of people taking brave risks for people they have never met, and in the majority of cases simply respond that they only did what anyone else would have done.

There are a number of factors that can influence how courageous we might be in any given situation. Courage is not, research tells us,[2] dependent on personality, but we may be more likely to be courageous for the sake of others if we are highly empathic; particularly, for example, in something like speaking up for others who have suffered injustice. The ultimate example of this is Jesus, identifying with a wounded world and, from deep love, taking the path to the cross with the most extraordinary display of courage.

An additional factor is training, skills and experience. A nurse dealing with a dangerous situation in an A and E department still needs courage, but the training they have received will make a difference, because they will have procedures to follow and may have faced similar situations before. We may not have particular training, but if we imagine what we might do in a difficult situation, or have a sense of identity that means we believe we are the kind of person who would exhibit bravery, this may contribute to us being able to do so should the need arise.

There have been many people of faith over the centuries who have displayed deep courage emanating from their faith in Jesus, from Stephen, who we will consider in a later chapter, through to the extraordinary courage currently being shown by many Christians choosing to remain in the Ukraine to help others as the war with Russia takes place. Mary had no training or experience to help her as she was called to demonstrate the most phenomenal courage. I have sometimes wondered if she was the first person to whom the angelic messenger was sent. Could anyone else have been approached who, unlike Mary, would not accept this unique and terrifying calling? Perhaps not, but what we do know is that this young girl found courage deep within herself which we cannot even begin to imagine. Her final words to the angel give us the answer to the source of that bravery. 'I am the Lord's servant,' she declares. Amid what must have been rising terror at all that lay ahead, she chose to look to God and place her trust in him as she served him in this unique way. Courage indeed.

Reflection questions

- Are there any examples of courageous people you admire?
- What are the times in your life that you have needed courage?
- Where do you see courage in the life of Jesus?

12

Simeon: Patience

Now there was a man in Jerusalem called Sim-
eon, who was righteous and devout. He was
waiting for the consolation of Israel, and the
Holy Spirit was on him.

Luke 2:25

The voice of Simeon

It had been such a long, long wait and at times I grew weary.
I longed to see God visit our people again, as he had of old.
I held on to the promises of the prophets that one day the
Messiah would come, that God had yet more for us. That we
would finally be the blessing to all peoples that was our calling
and from which we had fallen so very far.

I was a small child when the Romans first came to Jerusalem.
As I grew, all I could see was our people in pain, oppressed as
much as in the days of exile, almost worse now because it was
here, in our own nation, a land no longer feeling like home
with soldiers in the streets and tax collectors robbing us on
every corner. Many people, I knew, stopped believing in God
and allowed their hearts to fill with bitterness.

But I could not abandon my Creator. He had always been faithful to me, so why should I abandon him? I held on, sometimes so very falteringly, to what I believed he had said to me long before, that I would see the Messiah before I was laid to rest. As I aged, I often felt as though time was running out, yet still I waited. Each day I would whisper a prayer: 'Is it today, *Adonai?*' Every day, nothing. Nothing, until that day. That day was different.

I had been standing to pray, my old bones protesting with the customary stiffness of age. Almost by rote, expecting nothing, I said again, 'Is it today, *Adonai?*' I waited for the answering silence but instead, deep within my spirit I heard the words I had almost lost hope of hearing: 'Yes, today. Go to the temple.'

I paused for a moment. Had I misheard? Had my desperate longing created an inner thought that was entirely mine and not God's? Yet the impression, like a hand resting gently on my spirit, would not let me go. And so, unsure whether I felt hopeful or foolish, I hurried off to the temple courts.

Pausing, I looked around. As usual there was a sea of faces, everyone intent on the different reasons they had come: to pray, to worship, to make an offering. There seemed to be nothing for me to see here.

Again, I had a moment of doubt. Perhaps I should return home. I decided to look for one last time. And then I saw them. They were at that moment entering the temple, on the face of it just an ordinary couple, walking slowly and carefully, and as I looked more closely, I realised they were carrying a tiny baby, I assumed to present him to the Lord as our law required. Hesitating, I walked towards them, unsure what I would say, and stopped in front of them. The man looked questioningly at me, but then, as I held out my arms he passed the baby to me, seeming to understand that I meant no harm but only to bless, while his wife watched silently with eyes full of a wisdom which went beyond her years.

Words poured from me, words I had not rehearsed, words of thanks that at last, at last he was here, that my waiting had been vindicated and God had sent us the Rescuer he promised, not only for us but for all people, for the humanity he loves.

I could see they were trying to take in my words and, returning their precious son to his mother, I raised my hand for a final blessing on them. As I did so I felt my heart lurch, and I could see, dimly but with such certainty, a tiniest glimpse of the way ahead and the triumph and sorrow it would entail, and the cost for this young woman who stood in front of me with so much love in her eyes.

But that is for others to see, a story that they will need to tell. For me, I sense it will not be long now. My long wait is over, and I am content.

Luke 2 tells part of his story:

Now there was a man in Jerusalem called Simeon, who was righteous and devout. He was waiting for the consolation of Israel, and the Holy Spirit was on him. It had been revealed to him by the Holy Spirit that he would not die before he had seen the Lord's Messiah. Moved by the Spirit, he went into the temple courts. When the parents brought in the child Jesus to do for him what the custom of the Law required, Simeon took him in his arms and praised God, saying:

'Sovereign Lord, as you have promised,
you may now dismiss your servant in peace.
For my eyes have seen your salvation,

which you have prepared in the sight of all nations:
a light for revelation to the Gentiles,
and the glory of your people Israel.'

The child's father and mother marvelled at what was said about
him. Then Simeon blessed them and said to Mary, his mother:
'This child is destined to cause the falling and rising of many in
Israel, and to be a sign that will be spoken against, so that the
thoughts of many hearts will be revealed. And a sword will pierce
your own soul too.'

(Luke 2:25–35)

Exploration of patience

As I write this book, there are building works going on in our
home, which we moved to some six months ago. My study is
full of the contents of our (currently demolished) garage, and
walking to our small back garden entails clambering over rub-
ble. I am learning the limits of my patience!

The quality of patience is the one we use when we need
to wait for something, or to persist in a difficult situation or
with a complex task, and do so without anger or complaint.
In many ways it is the foil to frustration, which is a daily experience: a flight is delayed, a builder does not turn up, a call
we are expecting does not materialise, or we have to live with
ongoing pain. I am sure you can name your own challenges.
Impatience is perhaps particularly an issue in the West, where
so much is instant. We have twenty-four-hour access to information courtesy of the internet, and we can even see if a message on a mobile phone has been read, raising expectations of a

swift reply. Particularly in cities, the pace of life is rapid and the expectation is that everything else will match it.

Patience can be misunderstood as passivity, or even victim-hood: simply mentally lying down and letting circumstances walk over us. Or at times, it can be used as a way to nullify legitimate feelings of injustice in others that need to be heard. However, true biblical patience is not those things. Instead, it involves waiting for a reason, and at times enduring, with an underlying trust in God.[1]

How we can increase our capacity for patience depends on the particular areas where we are aware that we are challenged, and so the first step is to reflect on what the characteristics are in others, or particular situations, that make it most difficult for us to be patient. It is a feature of our psychology that we are often impatient towards the aspects of others that we also carry within ourselves, and it can be enlightening sometimes to ask ourselves, when struggling with impatience, if that is the case.

One helpful step, once we have recognised the particular triggers to our impatience, is to check where our focus lies in those situations. When we become irritated, for example, when a shop employee is slow, our focus tends to be inward: 'This is a waste of *my* time.' Patience may be easier if we can find an out-ward focus: 'It must be a difficult job in this heat.' This does not mean excusing poor service or other things which may need to be challenged, but recognising that there will certainly be other dimensions to a situation than the impact on us. Someone I know well recently said to me they had noticed they were inter-rupting others a lot: perhaps a flaw some of us can identify with as we jump prematurely into a conversation. They realised it was disrespectful and were working consciously on pausing, be-ing patient to allow the person to finish and for the dialogue to be unhurried. It is interesting that they were helped to practise patience by looking outward, at the effect on the other person.

I mention later, in the chapter about Herod and insecurity, the significance of self-talk. When we are faced with a situation which frustrates us, monitoring our self-talk can be helpful. There is a big difference between 'This is very annoying, this always happens to me' and, 'This is very annoying, but it is just one aspect of my day today.' It is important to acknowledge what we feel, but having done so, to put it in a wider context which will help us tolerate the delay or the situation, rather than enter a potentially negative spiral.

It can be helpful, in this as in other areas, to recognise the impact of past patterns, particularly during our upbringing, on us. It does appear that some people are inherently more patient than others, and as with all aspects of our personality, there is probably a mix of nature and nurture, genetics and life experiences, including what has been modelled to us. The former we can do nothing about, but the effect of the latter we can subvert, the starting place being an awareness of what we have witnessed, both in our growing years and since, and the impact it has had on us. Of course, if our impatience results in extreme anger or behaviour we cannot control, then it is vital to seek professional help.

At the time of the birth of Jesus, Simeon had been waiting a long time, and so had Israel. God, it seemed, had been silent since the prophet Malachi some 600 years before. Before that, there were longstanding promises of a Messiah, or 'Anointed one' – a title coming from the Jewish practice of anointing kings and priests, and found in various passages such as Psalm 2 and Daniel 9. This hope must have been both difficult to hold on to, and yet a source of optimism in the troubled and uncertain times under Roman rule.

Of course, Simeon was not the only biblical character to have experience of waiting. Hebrews 6:15 says of Abraham, 'so after waiting patiently, Abraham received what was promised'; however, his willingness to go ahead with the plan of Sarah to use her slave Hagar to produce a son instead might suggest the writer of Hebrews was being generous in their assessment. David waits for a considerable time and endures many difficulties before the anointing by Samuel finds its fulfilment when he finally becomes king.[2] Biblical women, including Hannah and Elizabeth, are described as waiting for a child, remaining faithful despite the suffering that their situation would have caused. These accounts can be a source of encouragement during times of waiting which can challenge our patience, particularly if we are waiting for something we believe is God's plan for us. There is, of course, no guarantee that our waiting patiently will result in what we hope for, only that in the waiting God does not leave us or forsake us.[3]

In addition to times of waiting, there are a number of situations in which the Bible urges us to exercise patience. These include times of difficulty or affliction,[4] perhaps the most demanding of all seasons in which to be patient. The attitudes of Christians who are suffering in places where the church is persecuted, or in war situations such as the Ukrainian church during the war with Russia, are humbling to those of us whose lives are smoother, but many of us will know individuals whose stories will never be known but who are quietly faithful in times of personal loss, pain or illness. We are equally told to continue patiently in 'doing good',[5] and in our relationships with each other,[6] bearing in mind that we are living in the light of eternity.[7]

Patience is seen as an integral quality of God himself. Specifically, on many occasions God is referred to as 'slow to anger'.[8] Paul's beautiful and well-known description of love in

1 Corinthians 13 is often considered as being ultimately a description of God whose very nature is love, and 'love is patient'.[9] The biblical account is that God is indeed patient with us, and Jesus modelled this in his patience with his disciples who were often confused, and then at the time of his greatest need, abandoned him. Paul elsewhere asserts that patience is an aspect of the fruit of the Spirit.[10] This link would suggest that perhaps the most significant way in which we can develop more patience is to cooperate with the work of the Spirit in our lives, as the psalmist expresses it, to 'Be still before the LORD and wait patiently for him'[11] and allow him to continue his patient transformation of us so that we begin to look a little more like Jesus.

Reflection questions

- What are the circumstances under which you find it easy, or less easy, to be patient?
- Who are the Bible characters who encourage you in this area?
- What have you learned from the examples around you, both in the past and today?

The Samaritan Woman: Witness

*'Come, see a man who told me everything I've
ever done. Could this be the Messiah?'*

John 4:29

The voice of the woman

It was so hot. I hated those midday trips to the well, always on
the alert, trying to lift the heavy water jar unaided up on to my
head for the journey back. But the lonely trek when the day was
hottest was preferable to the stares of the women in the early
morning, the way they turned their backs with disgust. I had
tried to join them once. Never again. It is so easy to judge when
you do not know the whole story, but I was too worn down to
try to explain to anyone. I would simply go on, day after day,
showing a brazen exterior which masked my aching heart.

As I approached, I saw the traveller. He was sitting on the
capstone, and I waited for him to move away as I approached.
But he didn't. He looked worn out, yet he was looking at me
intently in a way I should have found unnerving, but instead
found somehow intriguing.

I stood on the other side of the well, unsure what to do next. And then he spoke. 'Will you give me a drink of water?' His accent gave him away – he was a Jew! What was he doing here? Yes, we were the quickest route from Judea to Galilee but few came that way, fearing the old hostilities would break out in more than words. Why was he travelling alone, with no means of drawing water? He must have heard the shock in my voice as, trying to stay calm, I questioned him. 'Really? You are a Jew and I am a Samaritan woman. Our nations do not mix and nor do our genders.' After all, he would not want to drink from any container I had touched and defile his Jewish laws, surely. He held my gaze, seeming unaffected by either my tone or my words, instead saying if I knew who he was, I would ask him for living water. Now I was really confused. This well held water that rose from the ground, not stream water. What source of fresh, moving water did he have access to? It seemed impossible, but how wonderful would that be? No more arduous hot trips to this well . . .

'How?' I asked him. 'You do not even have a traveller's skin bucket!' I was confused and felt the need to proudly remind him it was our father Jacob who gave us the well. If this Jewish rabbi – for surely that was who he must be – was going to make claims, I was going to stand up for my people.

He didn't want to debate nationalities with me, though. 'This water only temporarily quenches thirst,' he said. 'The water I give will be a spring of water welling up to eternal life.' Now two very different emotions were rising up inside me. One was a sense that he was either deluded, or mocking me. What exactly was he offering? Something that would save me from this daily grind? Somehow, I began to sense, just on the very edge of my mind, that he was meaning something else. Something good amid my sad existence. So my reply to him was laced with a mixture of both cynicism and longing. 'Yes, please . . . so that I will never get thirsty and won't have to keep coming here.'

There was a kindness in his face at his next words, though they stung me. 'Go and fetch your husband.' Shame swept over me, even hotter than the midday sun, and I no longer looked at him but stared at the ground. I thought about simply walking away with no water. All those years, the repeated disasters of my personal life, flashed through my memories in an instant. The painful mixture of my failings and the rejections by others which had brought me here, somehow so exposed, talking with this stranger in the midday sun. Haltingly, hoping he could sense nothing of the maelstrom within, I said simply, 'I have no husband,' wishing that would be enough of an answer to satisfy him. His next answer shocked me to the very core. 'No, you don't. You have had five husbands and the man you now have is not your husband.' I wanted to glance at him, but could not fully meet his eyes. How did he know? Surely no one would have told this traveller? Was he more than a rabbi? A prophet, like Moses in our Pentateuch? What else could he see in me? I had so many questions.

We spoke for a long time as piece by piece he unpacked my wretched life. It was as if he saw beyond my story to the very deepest recesses of my soul. All the dashed hopes and broken dreams, all the fear and humiliation. He missed nothing, yet somehow, unlike everyone I had ever met, there was not condemnation but instead understanding, mercy even. I was both drawn to him and profoundly troubled. In the end, unsure what to do, I took refuge in the age-old disagreement about where worship belonged: our Mount Gerizim or their Jerusalem. There was almost a smile in his eyes as he gently bantered with me: 'You don't have all the story. There will come a time when worship is beyond either, a worship in spirit and truth of God who is the Spirit.'

Suddenly, it was as if I could see something so much bigger, a vista somehow opening up in front of me. Could he be our Taheb, the Converter, the one who was coming to make everything new, to restore everything to how it was meant to be? Unsure, I said quietly, hesitatingly, 'When the Messiah comes, he will tell us everything.'

For the first time, the stranger rose to his feet. All the weariness I had sensed in him seemed to have dissipated like morning mist. With a new authority I had never seen in any man, his words rang clear. 'I am he.' I stared at him as realisation dawned.

Just then his companions returned. I sensed their uncertainty, perhaps even disapproval, but they said nothing to him or (of course) to me. No matter. I had news to tell, and nothing was going to stop me telling it. I almost ran back, a new lightness and confidence in my steps. No shame from the past was going to stop me now.

It was only later, when I returned with most of my village, that I realised I had left my water jar behind.

John 4 tells her story:

Now Jesus learned that the Pharisees had heard that he was gaining and baptising more disciples than John – although in fact it was not Jesus who baptised, but his disciples. So he left Judea and went back once more to Galilee.

Now he had to go through Samaria. So he came to a town in Samaria called Sychar, near the plot of ground Jacob had given to his son Joseph. Jacob's well was there, and Jesus, tired as he was from the journey, sat down by the well. It was about noon.

When a Samaritan woman came to draw water, Jesus said to her, 'Will you give me a drink?' (His disciples had gone into the town to buy food.)

The Samaritan woman said to him, 'You are a Jew and I am a Samaritan woman. How can you ask me for a drink?' (For Jews do not associate with Samaritans.)

Jesus answered her, 'If you knew the gift of God and who it is that asks you for a drink, you would have asked him and he would have given you living water.'

'Sir,' the woman said, 'you have nothing to draw with and the well is deep. Where can you get this living water? Are you greater than our father Jacob, who gave us the well and drank from it himself, as did also his sons and his livestock?'

Jesus answered, 'Everyone who drinks this water will be thirsty again, but whoever drinks the water I give them will never thirst. Indeed, the water I give them will become in them a spring of water welling up to eternal life.'

The woman said to him, 'Sir, give me this water so that I won't get thirsty and have to keep coming here to draw water.'

He told her, 'Go, call your husband and come back.'

'I have no husband,' she replied.

Jesus said to her, 'You are right when you say you have no husband. The fact is, you have had five husbands, and the man you now have is not your husband. What you have just said is quite true.'

'Sir,' the woman said, 'I can see that you are a prophet. Our ancestors worshipped on this mountain, but you Jews claim that the place where we must worship is in Jerusalem.'

'Woman,' Jesus replied, 'believe me, a time is coming when you will worship the Father neither on this mountain nor in Jerusalem. You Samaritans worship what you do not know; we worship what we do know, for salvation is from the Jews. Yet a time is coming and has now come when the true worshippers will worship the Father in the Spirit and in truth, for they are the kind of worshippers the Father seeks. God is spirit, and his worshippers must worship in the Spirit and in truth.'

The woman said, 'I know that Messiah' (called Christ) 'is coming. When he comes, he will explain everything to us.'

Then Jesus declared, 'I, the one speaking to you – I am he.'

Just then his disciples returned and were surprised to find him talking with a woman. But no one asked, 'What do you want?' or 'Why are you talking with her?'

Then, leaving her water jar, the woman went back to the town and said to the people, 'Come, see a man who told me everything I've ever done. Could this be the Messiah?' They came out of the town and made their way towards him.

(John 4:1–30)

Exploration of witness

I love this story. There is something beautiful in Jesus' dealings with this woman, who one speaker once referred to as 'the town tart', an extraordinary mixture of compassion and challenge, which draws us in. As in other stories,[1] Jesus places reaching out to this woman, and through her to the whole village, ahead of the religious laws and social customs of his day. As she responds, she becomes the first evangelist to the Samaritans, a foretaste of the barriers that were to be even more fully broken down as in the early church the good news of the death and resurrection of Jesus spread to Samaritans and then to Gentiles.[2]

It is hard for us, at this distance, to fully grasp the deep enmity which existed between Jews and Samaritans, which went back hundreds of years. In 722BC the Assyrian Empire overcame the northern kingdom, deported the Israelites and repopulated the area with captives from other countries. The result was a hybrid religion with elements of the worship of Yahweh being mixed with the worship of Baal and the gods of the new inhabitants. After the inhabitants of Judah returned from exile in 539BC, there were already differences in both religion and politics with the people of Samaria, which were exacerbated when the Samaritans opposed the rebuilding of the walls of Jerusalem in the time of Nehemiah.[3] Later, in the time of the Maccabees, the Samaritans dedicated their temple on Mount Gerizim to the Greek god Zeus Xenios. By the time of Jesus, there was permanent and profound hostility between the two groups, with Jews seeing any contact with Samaritans as defiling, which is one of the reasons that the story of the Good Samaritan[4] was so powerful and shocking to the original Jewish hearers. Although the journey through Samaria would have been the quickest route between Galilee and Judea – for example, to attend the major festivals in Jerusalem – many avoided it because harassment from the Samaritans was not uncommon.

The well of Jacob, which is still there today, was at the foot of Mount Gerizim. The Samaritans justified their claim that Mount Gerizim should be the centre of worship by saying that Moses commanded the people, when entering the Promised Land, that curses and blessings be declared from Mount Ebal and Mount Gerizim respectively – thus declaring Mount Gerizim a place of blessing.[5] They did not acknowledge the temple at Jerusalem which was so important to Jews.

In the middle of these complex and heated political and religious debates Jesus, as a Jewish male rabbi, breaks all taboos by entering into conversation with this lonely woman, refusing to be sidetracked by her reticence about her domestic arrangements or her theological diversions. We don't know, of course, why she had five husbands. Some at least could have died, although multiple marriages, even due to death, were slightly frowned on by the rabbis. She may have been divorced, which in the culture of the day would not have been her doing as only men could divorce their wives and not vice versa, and it often happened on minor pretexts. However, given the fact that she came alone out of the village to the well at midday, rather than either going to the village well or coming out to this one with a group of women in the cooler morning, we can assume that she was very much on the fringes of village life.

I suspect that the account we have is a summary of a much longer conversation: this would explain her comment that Jesus has told her everything she has ever done. Whatever the exact details, the result is that she abandons her water pot to bring the villagers, presumably including those she was previously avoiding, to Jesus. We can assume that there was much in her life that still needed sorting out, and that her understanding was not yet complete: but she still wanted to bring people to meet Jesus for themselves. He had seen the very worst about her and, unlike the responses she must have experienced from others, accepted her. As a result, her first, compelling instinct, was to bring others to meet him. She was no longer to be shamed into seclusion: she had news to share.

Sharing faith in Jesus – witnessing, as it is often called – has been part of the Christian faith from the beginning. Matthew's gospel ends with the words: 'All authority in heaven and on earth has been given to me. Therefore go and make disciples of all nations, baptising them in the name of the Father and of the Son and of the Holy Spirit, and teaching them to obey everything I have commanded you. And surely I am with you always, to the very end of the age.'[6] Some, later, manuscripts of Mark's gospel include the similar words 'Go into all the world and preach the gospel to all creation'.[7] At the beginning of the book of Acts, the last words of Jesus before his ascension are recorded in this way: 'you will receive power when the Holy Spirit comes on you; and you will be my witnesses in Jerusalem, and in all Judea and Samaria, and to the ends of the earth.'[8]

When we hear the word 'witness' we are initially likely to think of a witness to a crime or in a court of law. I have done two stints of jury service, one of which was a six-week trial, and I can still remember the very close attention we paid to trying to assess the veracity of the witnesses. This use of the word in a court context is also found in the Old Testament, where being a witness is treated with great seriousness. Two or three witnesses were required to convict anyone of an offence, and the penalties for giving a false testimony, in breach of the ninth commandment, were severe.[9]

In a broader sense, Israel as a whole was seen as a living witness to the other nations around them of the splendour of God: '"You are my witnesses," declares the LORD, "that I am God."'[10] When individually or corporately rescued in some way, again they were to share that with others: 'Let the redeemed of the LORD tell their story – those he redeemed from the hand of the foe'.[11]

The apostles too emphasised that they were witnesses to the events they were describing, with John declaring, 'That which was from the beginning, which we have heard, which we have seen with our eyes, which we have looked at and our hands have touched – this we proclaim concerning the Word of life.'[12] He makes clear that this proclaiming, bearing witness to, is so that others come to faith.[13] It is clear from the earlier words of Jesus that this was to be more than words. He describes his disciples and their community as being like salt and light,[14] living out a demonstration of what it means to be the people of God. Paul uses a different yet linked image of Christians as ambassadors for Christ, representing him.[15] Paul makes clear that his own witness was not through eloquence: in contrast it was in weakness yet with the power of Christ and the simple yet life-changing message of the cross and resurrection.[16]

I suspect, however, that for many of us the idea of witnessing, of sharing our faith in Christ with others, is still difficult, even though many classic books on discipleship have a section on the subject as a basic element of the Christian life.[17] This may be because we have seen it done in ways which we feel are unhelpful, such as the doom-laden placard on Hyde Park corner or the individual shouting about hell and damnation in the shopping centre. It may be that our personality type or our gifting means it is more of a struggle – I can think of some people who talk about Jesus with great ease wherever they are, and I admire them greatly, but as a shy introvert I find it difficult.

So, what are the aspects of this remarkable story that can help us as we seek to be good witnesses to our faith? Let's consider a few.

The first starting point is where the story begins. We cannot tell whether Jesus has gone there deliberately, knowing that this woman will be there and seeking to have conversation with her, or whether he simply takes advantage of the fact she arrives at the well to reach out to her. However, clearly he literally comes to her space and meets her where she is. There has been an increasing move in recent years to move away from expecting people to come to church services or events, to come, as it were, into our space, but instead to be a presence where people are, with initiatives such as Alpha courses held in coffee shops or pubs. At an individual level, it can often feel more natural to talk as we are engaged in some other activity. A previous colleague of mine started regularly going to the local pub and has built a real ministry there sharing life and conversation, and as a result has been able to share his faith.

Once the woman had arrived, Jesus started by asking her for a drink. John makes clear this was not a ploy – he really was tired, hot and thirsty from walking in the heat of the day. He started from a place of his own need and vulnerability. Sometimes people have expressed to me that they cannot talk to others about Jesus because there are still aspects of their lives which are not perfect. That would disqualify all of us. I don't think that others expect perfection from Christians, but the illusion that we are, or think we are, somehow better than others can linger and so creates an unhelpful distance. Sometimes it can be really helpful to allow others to help us, as Jesus did. It is a beneficial attitude to foster in any case: we are most whole when we can both give and receive, rather than only give out to others. To allow others to help us also elevates their self-worth, which in the case of this woman was clearly much needed.

As we saw earlier, Jesus was unafraid to breach convention in order to help this woman, a feature throughout his ministry. There was no sense for him of people who were appropriate for him to reach out to and others who weren't. While he was acerbic at times in his criticism of the religious leaders,[18] he ate with them too,[19] an important measure of acceptance in his culture. It can be so easy for us to feel some groups or individuals are unreachable, yet clearly this was never Jesus' attitude.

Jesus took the woman's questions seriously, even though perhaps at moments they were a mixture of genuine curiosity, even bewilderment, alongside a desire to deflect from her personal situation. He did not necessarily answer them directly, but her questions were an important part of the conversation, a starting point for what he wanted to share. As Christians we need, I believe, to allow both ourselves and others to ask questions.

We do not have to have all the answers neatly worked out to witness to others: quite the contrary, asking them, and us sharing our own, may be an important part of the process in someone's life. We need what the minister at our current church calls 'honest faith'; at times holding in one hand our questions and, yes, our doubts, and in the other our faith.

Perhaps the most marked aspect not just of this encounter but of the whole of Jesus' ministry is the respect, compassion and love with which Jesus dealt with those he encountered. The broken and the outcast were naturally drawn to him and he was unafraid to be seen with them.[20] Any attempt to witness which is lacking in those features will be not only doomed to failure but actively damaging. It is so sad that so much harm is done in the witness of both individuals and the church if the prevalent attitude is judgement. In contrast, Jesus indicated that 'by this everyone will know that you are my disciples, if you love one another'.[21] If love for one another was a witness in itself, then surely love for others must be too.

Finally, what of this remarkable woman? In what ways can she help us think about our witness? One of the things that strikes me is her sheer excitement. She was so keen to get back to her village that she left her water pot behind. Often new Christians are much more able to witness enthusiastically because their faith is so fresh and they have the joy of newly discovering Jesus. The challenge for those of us who have been Christians longer is to retain that same spontaneity. She also did not allow her past, that shame which had brought her to the well alone at noon, to hold her back. She had discovered in Jesus, unformed and fledgling though her faith undoubtedly was, something that was simply too good not to be shared. She has much to teach us, reminding us to continually find again the joy and amazement of that initial, life-changing, discovery.

Reflection questions

- Are there times when people have witnessed to you about their faith? Was what you heard a part of your faith journey?
- How easy, or difficult, do you find it to talk to others about Jesus?
- What do you think are the things which make our witness more, or less, effective?

14

The Widow: Generosity

He also saw a poor widow put in two very small copper coins.

Luke 21:2

The voice of the widow

I was a little nervous as I entered the temple that day. I always felt so small, surrounded by all those important men making their way through our court, the Court of the Women, to their areas beyond. Among them were the priests and the Levites, those godly men who led the worship on our behalf and told us how to live, who interpreted God's beautiful Law. I am so very ordinary.

It had been so hard since my Benjamin died. I missed him, still do, more than I can say. The nights felt cold and the days dreary without those shared smiles: oh, how I had loved his laugh as he teased me. It was my greatest sadness that there were no children to remind me of him. It meant that I was reliant on what I could glean, such as the olives left for those of us in need after the landowner at Gethsemane had taken the first harvest. I would press them, hard work with Benjamin's old wooden mallet, but the paste and the oil could be sold in the local market. It was a simple life.

But I knew God had promised that he would sustain me, as he did all of us in my circumstance. Sometimes, when I woke in the night, I would remember the widow of Zarephath and I would ask God to help me as he had helped her. He is faithful, and always, when I had times I was afraid, somehow there was just enough. I had learned to trust him.

So that day was a special day. God had blessed the olive trees and there was more than usual. I had two lepta left over after purchasing grain and provisions from my sales at the market. My friend said I should keep them for leaner times: what if next time the olive crop failed? But I knew what I wanted to do. So I found myself there, in front of The Trumpets. I glanced around, and saw a rabbi sitting there. His head was bowed, resting in his hands as if with weariness. He looked up, and I turned away in respect. Glancing back at The Trumpets, I briefly studied all thirteen, though I knew exactly which one I was going to put my coins in: the one where the money goes to incense to be burned on the altar. It was such a small amount, but it thrilled me to think that, as the fragrance of the incense filled the temple, as worship rose and the prayers it represented reached God, I would have played a tiny part.

He had given me so much, and my heart was filled with joy as I gently dropped in the coins.

The Gospel of Luke tells her story:

As Jesus looked up, he saw the rich putting their gifts into the temple treasury. He also saw a poor widow put in two very small copper coins. 'Truly I tell you,' he said, 'this poor widow has put in more than all the others. All these people gave their gifts out of their wealth; but she out of her poverty put in all she had to live on.'

(Luke 21:1–4)

Exploration of generosity

We exhibit generosity when we give more of something than might be expected. It is important to remember that although generosity is often associated with money, there are many other ways it can be expressed, such as the gifting of time or practical help. For many years I ran a low-cost counselling service in the community. While many clients came with complex psychological issues needing skilled help, some simply needed good, unselfish listening, where there is no interruption or switching the focus to the story of the listener. There is so little of that generous listening in everyday life. In our fraught, 24/7 life in the West, the gift of time can also be immensely precious. During a difficult spell in my life, someone regularly gave up their time to walk in a park with me, which was a gift that meant a great deal. Recently I was talking to someone who was describing the way a colleague worked with them, and she called it 'generous hands' – an expression I loved and which referred to several different elements in their working relationship. Generosity is like a multifaceted diamond with a number of expressions.

For the widow, the money she gave was generous, far more than might have been expected for someone living permanently at a subsistence level. The words of Jesus imply that this financial gift expressed a generosity of heart and spirit. By any gauge, the offering brought by this widow was a tiny one – it equated to just five minutes labour at minimum wage. Yet Jesus made clear that in reality hers was a far more generous gift than those of the others who, from their abundance, were tossing multiple coins into the temple offerings.

The Old Testament stipulated the giving of a tithe, or 10 per cent, of a person's possessions as an expression of faith and as part of the provision both for the poor, and also for the Levites, to free them to serve God.[1] Not just money was included, but all crops and animals. To skimp or cheat on this was treated with great seriousness, as tantamount to robbing God,[2] and generosity was seen as bringing blessing.[3] Tithing is not commanded in the New Testament: in fact, Jesus had sharp words of criticism for those who tithed the tiniest thing yet did not have the same concern for ensuring justice or practising mercy.[4] Provision was made, however, for those in need 'as each one was able'[5] and the attitude with which it was given was important, so that anything given was done so cheerfully and not grudgingly.[6] This same link between generosity and blessing, in this case the context suggesting generosity in forgiveness, is found in Jesus' teaching: 'Give, and it will be given to you. A good measure, pressed down, shaken together and running over, will be poured into your lap. For with the measure you use, it will be measured to you.'[7] We will return to the subject of forgiveness in Chapter 19.

Interestingly, the concept and practice of generosity has been studied in a number of fields, including neuroscience, psychology and sociology. Studies have shown that some species do act in the interests of others, for example female vampire bats who share their food with other roosting bats who need extra nutrition.[8] It is, however, unlikely that many species are capable of altruism or empathy, which suggests in those instances there is some in-built instinct, ultimately linked to the survival of the colony or group. In more advanced species, such as elephants and particularly primates, there is a stronger social bond and, unusually, emotion and empathy.[9] What other species do not possess, however, as far as we can tell, is the capacity or willingness to give generously or act on behalf of those with whom they have no connection. This appears to be a purely human trait.

As people of faith, the starting point for any of our giving is what we have already received from God. Jesus sent his disciples out to share the good news with the words 'Freely you have received; freely give.'[10] As John expresses it, 'See what great love the Father has lavished on us, that we should be called children of God! And that is what we are!'[11] Our generosity springs from having received the generous love of God, expressed in creation, in the gift of life to us, and most of all in the sacrificial, self-giving life, death and resurrection of Jesus. We see this exemplified in the story of Zacchaeus, who in being found by Jesus, gave half of his possessions away, a much higher amount than the 20 per cent considered generous, and offered to repay those he had cheated four times over,[12] far above the fifth extra required by Jewish Law.[13]

Generosity needs to go hand in hand with sensitivity. We may want to give freely of our time, finances or other things, but this can be from our need to give, not from the perspective of the other person and what will help them. If what we wish to give is not what the other person wants or needs, then we may need to delay or even completely curtail our giving. Our giving must not disempower another or make them feel diminished.

It would appear that it genuinely is more pleasurable to give than to receive. One study showed that when given unexpected money, in different amounts, those who were instructed to give it away were happier at the end of the day than those who were told to spend it on themselves.[14] Another study linked this with specific neural pathways in the brain.[15] However, what is not so clear is whether it is the act of giving itself which brings us pleasure, or other gains such as the gratitude of others, a boost in our self-esteem, or the strengthening of social bonds.

We need to both give and receive to have truly balanced personalities and relationships. Imagine a pool which is fed by a stream at one end and flows out to another. If the first stream dried up, the pool will too. But if the outgoing stream is blocked, the pool will overflow or become stagnant. For some of us, being generous with our time, money and love is much easier than being on the receiving end of the generosity of others. As a result, sometimes such generous gifts, which would bless the giver if we receive them well, are 'batted off' with a less than gracious response, or even refused. The growing edge for some of us may not be in giving, but in receiving, and to receive well can itself be a generous and loving act.

Reflection questions

- What other examples of generosity can you think of from the Bible?
- Take some time to reflect on the generosity that you have received from people in your life.
- How easy do you find it to be generous in the different areas in your life: money, time, sharing skills, etc.?

15

Judas: Betrayal

And it was night.

John 13:30

The voice of Judas

My God, my God, what have I done? In heaven's name, what have I done?

These last few years have not been easy but they have been extraordinary, like nothing I have ever experienced before. I always wondered why Jesus chose me. They were all from the north, and I'm a southerner . . . and I always felt as though I never really belonged, was somehow on the edge. Yet I was so drawn to Jesus: to his teaching, yes, but most of all to who he is, something indefinable that captivated all of us, and made us all proud to be in his inner circle. We would surround him, seeing the crowds who flocked to him and knowing we had a place in his life that they did not. Yet even so, I felt on the fringe. I had such a passion for the poor, but believed the only way to help them was for us to overthrow the Romans, establish the rule that God had promised would come when his Messiah came. To listen to Jesus' teaching, to enjoy the miracles, to spread the news about him . . . it was wonderful, but it was not enough. Something more radical even than inspiring words was needed.

When I was given the job of holding the common purse I wondered if I had finally been accepted, yet even then I felt my every move was being scrutinised. In the end, yes, I took to quietly using some of the money for what I deemed the fighting fund, ready for the time when Jesus openly declared that he was Messiah. I thought that when that happened, I could hand over everything I had accrued, and at last I might be applauded, drawn right into the centre at last, there with his favourites Peter, James and John.

I was so sure that my plan would work. As soon as they came for him, those who had shouted for him on Yom Rishon[1] would surely rise up and fight. I've seen what he can do, witnessed the miracles: this, surely is our moment? I did not see it as a betrayal, but as a coming coronation which I would have helped to bring about.

The meal was difficult. At the start, no one offered to do the usual foot washing, and so Jesus did. It felt awkward, but more so when it was my turn. He seemed to take longer, wash more thoroughly somehow and with such gentleness. As the meal progressed, I was on edge, thinking about the fighting to come, wishing I could tell Jesus. The mood was tense, as if others knew my plan even though they couldn't have. Even more disturbingly, Jesus began to talk about betrayal. 'No, no, Jesus!' I wanted to shout. 'I am going to bring about your reign, your triumph! Can't you see? You will thank me, Jesus, you will.'

But, looking back, when he handed me the bread, it was as though a terrible darkness overwhelmed me. He looked at me with such tenderness, such love, as though he knew everything, all the wrestling and isolation of my three years with them, all my jealousy of the inner circle, everything that I despised within myself and loathed within others. It was as if I was naked, exposed in his gaze, and I was somehow angry. I would show him. I left, out into the pitch darkness.

I knew where he would go. His favourite place, Gethsemane. He loved to pray there. As I snaked my way through the trees with the soldiers, I had a brief moment of apprehension. Could I have got it wrong? But I brushed it aside. I would have my moment of glory, and so would Jesus.

In the gloom, to help the soldiers identify him, we had agreed I would kiss him in greeting. As I went to do so, just for a moment, he grasped me at arm's length. Again, like at the supper, he held my gaze. Again, and now the memory crushes me, he looked at me with such love. And, worst of all, his eyes were filled with tears.

All hell broke loose, but not as I had planned. There was no battle, no call to the citizens of Jerusalem and the Passover pilgrims to fight, no rout. Just the darkness, and Jesus, who at the very last had called me 'Friend', being led silently away.

I tried to put it right, but to no avail. I thought of going to find the disciples, but they would never have taken me back. It is over for me now.

My God, my God, what have I done? In heaven's name, what have I done?

Matthew and John's gospels tell part of his story:

Then one of the Twelve – the one called Judas Iscariot – went to the chief priests and asked, 'What are you willing to give me if I deliver him over to you?' So they counted out for him thirty pieces of silver. From then on Judas watched for an opportunity to hand him over.

. . . Jesus told him, 'What you are about to do, do quickly.' But no one at the meal understood why Jesus said this to him. Since

Judas had charge of the money, some thought Jesus was telling him to buy what was needed for the festival, or to give something to the poor. As soon as Judas had taken the bread, he went out. And it was night.

. . . While he was still speaking, Judas, one of the Twelve, arrived. With him was a large crowd armed with swords and clubs, sent from the chief priests and the elders of the people. Now the betrayer had arranged a signal with them: 'The one I kiss is the man; arrest him.' Going at once to Jesus, Judas said, 'Greetings, Rabbi!' and kissed him. Jesus replied, 'Do what you came for, friend.'

. . . Early in the morning, all the chief priests and the elders of the people made their plans how to have Jesus executed. So they bound him, led him away and handed him over to Pilate the governor. When Judas, who had betrayed him, saw that Jesus was condemned, he was seized with remorse and returned the thirty pieces of silver to the chief priests and the elders. 'I have sinned,' he said, 'for I have betrayed innocent blood.'

'What is that to us?' they replied. 'That's your responsibility.'

So Judas threw the money into the temple and left. Then he went away and hanged himself.

> (Matt. 26:14–16; John 13:27–30;
> Matt. 26:47–50; 27:1–5)

Exploration of betrayal

Betrayal. It is an ugly word, which describes an equally hideous action. Judas has come to represent betrayal and we even refer to 'a Judas' if we feel someone has been disloyal. Many have tried to work out why he betrayed Jesus, but the truth is we cannot know for sure.

Judas was a common name, but the name at that time would have made Jews think of Judas Maccabeus, a Jewish priest and revolutionary from the inter-testamental period and at the centre of a successful Jewish rebellion, part of which is commemorated in the festival of Hanukkah. Was Judas named after him and told of his exploits growing up? The name 'Iscariot' has a possible link with the Zealots, which does add to the possibility of a political motive.[2] Was it his misunderstanding of both the real purpose and the cost of Jesus' ministry, the inability to accept that the path for the Messiah would bring suffering, and the desire to prompt the battle he felt was inevitable the reason for his betrayal? Again, we do not know, but it is a plausible theory.

There are some things we do know. He was a southerner, in contrast to the other disciples. We don't know when or how he was called by Jesus, but he did follow and was a full part of the disciples right until that fateful night. When Jesus spoke of betrayal at the Last Supper, they did not all expectantly turn to Judas, but in contrast had no idea who Jesus meant. Judas was one of them, trusted even with the money they shared for provisions. We also know that the sum of money he was paid by the religious leaders was very small: it was the amount to be paid if a bull gored a slave and allowing for the time between this rule being set and Jesus' day, we can assume it had diminished in value.[3] It seems highly unlikely that the money he was paid was his motivation.

The other, deeply poignant, thing that we know is the profound effect on Jesus of the betrayal. In John 13:21 we read that 'Jesus was troubled in spirit'. It is the same phrase used in other places of agitation or disturbance.[4] It would seem that right to the end Jesus is seeking to reach out to Judas: he gives him the morsel at the supper which when given by the host was a mark of honour, as was being within arm's length of Jesus, presumably the case for Judas since Jesus could reach him with the portion of food.[5] Even at the point of arrest, Jesus says,

'Judas, are you betraying the Son of Man with a kiss?'[6] and calls him 'friend'.[7] It is deeply moving. We cannot tell if, had Judas, even at the last, pulled back he might have been saved from his own tragic end and another way found for Jesus to take the path to the cross. Or if Judas, like Peter after the denial, could have believed in and received the forgiveness of Jesus: a forgiveness which is without limit. Instead, in remorse for his terrible betrayal, he took his own life. There is an often-quoted and poignant story that a child, when asked where Jesus went between his death and resurrection, said he had gone to find his friend Judas.[8]

I have commented on how disturbing Jesus found his imminent betrayal: presumably it must also have been devastating for the disciples, who from their reaction at the Last Supper had clearly not anticipated it. As well as their agony at all that happened to Jesus, their pain must have been compounded by the fact that it had come about because of the actions of one of their own.

It is trust that lies at the heart of the particular pain of betrayal.[9] Trust is necessary for our functioning as people, from the trivial, such as trusting a chair to hold our weight, through to the highly significant, such as trusting people in our closest relationships. When we trust someone, for example by speaking to them in confidence about something that is troubling us, and that trust is betrayed, in that instance by what we shared being disclosed to someone else, the shock and distress we experience is profound. This is particularly the case where we are in a dependant relationship, such as between a child and parent. It is an additional reason, as well as the impact of the trauma itself, why sometimes experiences of abuse or other trauma are blocked out by what has been referred to as 'betrayal blindness'.[10]

There are, of course, many contexts in which betrayal can take place: the most common perhaps being the home (whether in childhood or adulthood), friendship and the workplace. In each of these we may trust others in different ways, and the closer the relationship the deeper the impact of the betrayal will be. Friendship is a particularly painful place to experience betrayal. Whether factually accurate or not, there is a deep sadness in the words Shakespeare attributes to Julius Caesar in the play of the same name, as his supposed friend literally stabs him in the back: 'Et tu, Brute', 'You too, Brutus?'[11]

Part of the impact of betrayal is that it can leave us questioning our own ability to judge people and situations accurately. Some years ago, I supported someone applying for promotion, which put them in authority over me in the workplace. Not long afterwards they betrayed my confidence in a matter of great sensitivity. It left me wondering why I had not spotted this element of their personality, as I usually see myself as a good judge of character, and I was wary afterwards of trusting not just that particular person but my own judgement.

Whether we experience an action as betrayal in any particular instance depends on our expectations and the norms of the relationship. When I was counselling, at the assessment I always pointed out the exceptions to confidentiality: put simply, if I believed the client or someone else to be at risk.[12] If I had ever had to breach confidentiality, which mercifully I didn't, it would have been quite possible and understandable for the client to have felt betrayed, even though in fact I would have been within the norms and 'rules' of a counselling relationship. Betrayal is sometimes clearcut but may at other times be subjective, particularly if the different people involved have dissimilar expectations which have not been expressed or explored. The pain will be equally deep even if that is the case. Indeed, when we encounter a betrayal there is a process of grieving where we experience similar emotions: numbness, denial, anger and so on.[13] One of the aspects of the loss we experience in a situation where we have been betrayed is of our self-esteem: feeling we were not valued enough for the person to care enough not to betray us. It can also, of course, make it more difficult to trust again in the future: we need to learn not to distrust everything and everyone, which can also damage our relationships, but to develop what can be called 'wise trust'.[14]

Catastrophic betrayals can impact us for a very long time, raising extremely difficult challenges in terms of how we should respond. Retaliation is not the biblical way, however much we might want to take that path: Paul exhorts us to 'not repay anyone evil for evil'.[15] Jesus of course taught that we should forgive[16] and we will come back to the complex issue of forgiveness in a later chapter. That forgiveness is something which, without doubt, Jesus would have gifted Judas, and it is part of the tragedy of the story that Judas was unable to give Jesus the opportunity.

Reflection questions

- Have you ever betrayed anyone? Have you been able to forgive yourself?
- Are there some examples in your life of being betrayed where God needs to bring some healing? Would it help to ask for help from someone you trust?
- What does Jesus' love for Judas, right to the end, say to you about the times you have let Jesus down?

Herod Antipas: Insecurity

When Herod saw Jesus, he was greatly pleased,
because for a long time he had been wanting to
see him.

Luke 23:8

The voice of Herod

He's finally standing in front of me. Jesus. After years of curiosity and rumours, he is here.

I'm not sure what I expected, but not this. He looks so . . . ordinary. Not like John. He was anything but ordinary. Wild, untamable, yet something about him fascinated me. I hated his preaching and what he said about me, of course. Who was he to tell me that Herodias and I were in the wrong? She and I laughed about it sometimes, mocking him in our bedchamber. I joined in with her, my voice scathing, yet a corner of me felt discomforted. Something about him drew me somehow, as though we were joined with an invisible thread I could not sever.

Most of the time I am not sure if I believe in God, or if I do, whether God would concern himself with my life and the choices I make. But there was a light in John's eyes, a fire that my cynicism could never extinguish. I used to go down to the prison sometimes, supposedly to check on the guards, but really so that I could look at him. We didn't speak, but he would fix me with a stare. I admired his certainty: a quality I had always lacked, though I worked hard to project the opposite to those around me. My building projects can never be as grand as those of my father and I don't produce intricate coins like my half-brother Philip. The people do not do badly under my rule, yet I know they hate me.

I still have nightmares about the day he died. That ridiculous promise to grant Salome anything she wanted, born of the foolishness of drink and the desire to impress the gathering. My heart sank as she walked towards her mother, guessing the horror to come. I did not want to give the order, everything within me knowing that nothing good could come of it. But as I scanned the expectant faces of the dignitaries around me, I felt I had no choice and so I made the order swiftly before my fears could delay me. I have not had a restful moment since.

And now, here is Jesus in front of me. I can't make him out. Is this John come back to punish me, as I have feared? I know it makes no logical sense, but I see that same fire in his eyes. Ever since I heard of Jesus I have been fascinated and repelled in equal measure. At times I have wanted to destroy him, especially when my spies told me he had called me a fox, so that both he and John would stop tormenting my thoughts. At other moments I have wondered if he really was the miracle worker people claimed. Here now is my chance, even though I suspect he is only here because Pilate is blame-shifting, uncertain what to do with this enigmatic rabbi.

But Jesus won't dance to my tune. In fact, I sense he does not dance to anyone's. There is a vulnerability about him as he stands there, at my mercy, yet also a peculiar calm and certainty which I envy. Seeing his demeanour, so different, reveals the insecurity which constantly threatens to come to the surface of my psyche, and so I start to ply him with questions. Come on Jesus, give me something. Call down some miracle. Show me there is a God.

Nothing. Simply silence as he holds my gaze; I cannot read what is in his eyes but, to my fury, it looks like pity. I won't be pitied. I am the tetrarch. *I* am somebody.

So my soldiers and I mock him, dressing him like a king. I am the loudest, jeering with as much venom as I can muster, and then send him back to Pilate. Let him see if he can make sense of him.

Yet, as I watch him go, I wonder . . .

The gospels tell part of his story:

. . . Jesus' name had become well known. Some were saying, 'John the Baptist has been raised from the dead, and that is why miraculous powers are at work in him.' Others said, 'He is Elijah.' And still others claimed, 'He is a prophet, like one of the prophets of long ago.'

But when Herod heard this, he said, 'John, whom I beheaded, has been raised from the dead!'

For Herod himself had given orders to have John arrested, and he had him bound and put in prison. He did this because of Herodias, his brother Philip's wife, whom he had married. For John had been saying to Herod, 'It is not lawful for you to have your brother's wife.' So Herodias nursed a grudge against John and wanted to kill him. But she was not able to, because Herod feared John and protected him, knowing him to be a righteous and holy man. When Herod heard John, he was greatly puzzled; yet he liked to listen to him.

Finally the opportune time came. On his birthday Herod gave a banquet for his high officials and military commanders and the leading men of Galilee. When the daughter of Herodias came in and danced, she pleased Herod and his dinner guests.

The king said to the girl, 'Ask me for anything you want, and I'll give it to you.' And he promised her with an oath, 'Whatever you ask I will give you, up to half my kingdom.'

She went out and said to her mother, 'What shall I ask for?'

'The head of John the Baptist,' she answered.

At once the girl hurried in to the king with the request: 'I want you to give me right now the head of John the Baptist on a dish.' The king was greatly distressed, but because of his oaths and his dinner guests, he did not want to refuse her. So he immediately sent an executioner with orders to bring John's head. The man went, beheaded John in the prison, and brought back his head on a dish. He presented it to the girl, and she gave it to her mother. On hearing of this, John's disciples came and took his body and laid it in a tomb . . .

On hearing this, Pilate asked if the man [Jesus] was a Galilean. When he learned that Jesus was under Herod's jurisdiction, he sent him to Herod, who was also in Jerusalem at that time.

When Herod saw Jesus, he was greatly pleased, because for a long time he had been wanting to see him. From what he had heard about him, he hoped to see him perform a sign of some sort. He plied him with many questions, but Jesus gave him no answer. The chief priests and the teachers of the law were standing there, vehemently accusing him. Then Herod and his soldiers ridiculed and mocked him. Dressing him in an elegant robe, they sent him back to Pilate. That day Herod and Pilate became friends – before this they had been enemies.

(Mark 6:14–29; Luke 23:6–12)

Exploration of insecurity

It is perhaps important to start our reflection with untangling
who this specific Herod was. Herod Antipas is actually one
of six Herods who are mentioned in the New Testament. His
father was Herod the Great, the infamous Herod who ordered
the killings of the children in Bethlehem.[1] Herod the Great was
a non-Jew, married to a Samaritan, appointed by the Roman
occupiers which added to the distrust in which he was held.
He was ruthless, executing two of his own sons, Alexander and
Aristobulus IV. He engaged in massive building projects funded
by heavy tax burdens imposed on the ordinary people. After his
death, control of Palestine was split between his sons Herod
Archelaus, Herod Antipas and Herod Philip. Herod Philip is
only mentioned once in the New Testament, as simply Philip,
in Mark 6:17. Archelaus was in charge of Judea, Samaria and
Idumea, though only briefly, and was then replaced by direct
rule from Caesar Augustus. It was for fear of him that Joseph
and Mary, returning from Egypt on the death of Herod the
Great, settled back in Galilee.[2] Herod Agrippa I (the nephew
of Herod Antipas) appears in Acts 12 and his son, Herod
Agrippa II, the last of the Herods to rule over Palestine, in Acts
26. Herod Antipas, who we are considering in this chapter,
ruled Galilee and Perea from 4BC to AD39 and is mentioned
more than any of the other Herods in the New Testament.[3]

Herod Antipas is a fascinating character; accounts of him
from both the Bible and other sources providing some insight
into the complexities of his personality. The ethnic mix of
his parents would have meant he was considered inferior in
a land where pure Jewish heritage was prized. His father, who
had ten wives in total, was a towering and callous personality, yet with many abilities, and those competencies and the

power of his persona must have been difficult to live up to.[4] In addition to the complex background of his family, Herod Antipas was educated in Rome, a city steeped in the cult of the emperor. His father originally named him sole successor but later retracted, and as a result Herod Antipas was deprived of the status of responsibility for the capital Jerusalem when the land was divided up.[5] This must have been both disappointing and a wound to his ego: various appeals to Rome, both then and later, yielded no results and he seems to have vacillated between acquiescence to authority and angry belligerence. He was a deeply unpopular figure. It was, of course, his marriage to his half-brother Philip's wife (who was also his niece)[6] that prompted the denunciation by John the Baptist with its tragic ramifications. There was nothing in Herod's background or life that would lead him to be other than suspicious and insecure.

Insecurity is the unsettling feeling we experience when, either in a particular situation or more generally, we lack confidence either in our capability or how we are seen by others. It is multifaceted and may either be generalised, or focused in particular areas such as physical abilities, mental capacities, or the emotional realm including relationships. A person may have insecurity and resultant anxiety in all areas of their life, or may have confidence in one area, for example, their intellectual capacity, but be insecure in another, such as their physical appearance. This may lead to overcompensating by focusing on one area and minimising another. There are a number of different aspects of our lives in which we can potentially feel insecure: we are going to look briefly at some of the most common.

The first area where we can experience insecurity is relationships. This will be a particular area of vulnerability if there have been difficulties in attachment in childhood, such as may occur if parenting has been disrupted by illness, absence, or abuse. However, it can also occur where there has been trauma in adult relationships, such as a partner leaving. If one partner in a relationship is insecure and exhibits this by clinging or controlling behaviour, this can itself lead to difficulties in the relationship, as the other person feels pressured and withdraws, creating a vicious circle of insecurity.

A second context in which insecurities can arise is social settings. Recently I went to a group meeting in an unfamiliar setting and felt totally lost. I am confident in familiar settings where I have a role, but the combination of my introversion and the new situation meant that on this occasion I felt profoundly insecure and almost left. Insecurity in social settings can be general, or only coming to the fore in particular settings or for particular reasons.

Body image is another way in which many people experience insecurity. This can be in relation to a number of areas such as weight, musculature and facial features, but can vary enormously. For some, for example, the results of ageing can be very difficult, particularly if aspects of youth, such as particular looks or physical fitness have been a source of the admiration of others or even income.

The school or workplace can sow seeds of insecurity. Again, this may be generalised, such as in the capacity we all have to experience 'imposter syndrome'. This concept, first named by clinical psychologists Pauline Clance[7] and Susanne Imes, refers to the feeling that we do not deserve, or are not equipped for, a role we carry and are in danger of being unmasked as a fraud.[8] Or the insecurity may be specific, such as when failing finances within an organisation mean redundancies are a possibility. In a school setting, poor academic performance in one area can lead to insecurity either in that area or more generally, exacerbated if there are over-critical styles of teaching. Criticism, especially if it is constant and not balanced by praise for good work or behaviour, can seriously undermine our sense of security and well-being. Those with additional needs, especially if they are undiagnosed or poorly supported, can particularly struggle in this area.

As I write this book, there is a cost-of-living crisis in the UK. When basic necessities such as food and shelter are threatened, insecurity is a likely result. As mentioned in Chapter 1, Abraham Maslow proposed a theory of motivation in which he described a hierarchy of needs. The most fundamental of these is the physiological. When it is unclear how these basic needs will be met, we will experience anxiety and a sense of insecurity about our future and potential well-being, specifically our ability to provide for these basic human needs for ourselves and any dependants.

Both life experiences and personality traits can also be a factor in developing insecurity. Failures, especially if recent, can lead to uncertainty when a similar situation is encountered. A singer who forgets words in an important concert will be potentially less sure of their abilities at the next. Experiences of being bullied, for example at school or in the workplace, are devastating and may lead to ongoing anxiety and insecurity. This is particularly sad because the bully may well be masking their own insecurities by their behaviour. At times insecurity is linked with perfectionism. This may be due to expecting too much of ourselves, or assuming that others expect impossible standards of us, resulting in a fear of disappointing them. This is more than setting high standards for ourselves or others, it is seeking to attain perfection, which is unattainable in an imperfect world.[9] Social media can be unhelpful here, portraying perfect lives or perfect bodies rather than a more realistic view of everyday life with all its flaws.

Underlying insecurity is not always obvious in the way it presents. In relationships it may exhibit in jealousy, controlling behaviour, or a constant checking on the relationship. In other contexts, insecurity may result in self-deprecating remarks, which may or may not be because the speaker is seeking reassurance. Alternatively, it can present as grandiose behaviour, an arrogant presentation which is masking what lies underneath. Insecurity in a work or educational setting can sometimes result in putting off tasks from fear of failure, which can in itself become problematic if the person fails to meet important deadlines.

It is arguable that insecurity is a universal experience, especially given the fact that we all experience limitations in some areas, in particular with regard to our mortality. For some, however, the insecurity is debilitating, either in one area or more generally. If that is the case, what are some of the ways in which we can address it?

The first step, as with any psychological issue, is to acknowledge that it is there. This is not always easy as we are all adept at seeing others more clearly than we see ourselves. It can be helpful to have those around us who will lovingly but honestly tell us what they can see if we cannot see it ourselves. Other people can also be helpful in reframing both our perceptions and our expectations of ourselves, including facilitating our realisation that although we may not be skilled in some areas we are in others, allowing us to take a more holistic look at ourselves and our story.

Having ascertained that we may be feeling insecure, the next step is, if possible, to work out whether the root is current, historical, or both. This can help in planning the next course of action. If the origin is in the past, can we look at our experiences differently in the present? For example, was that criticism we received as a child fair? If the origin is in the present, is it a situation we can change, such as learning a new skill, or might it be better to move on in some way? In all of this, our self-talk is very important. We each hold a kind of inner running commentary on our lives. If I stumble, I may say to myself a rather negative, 'Silly woman, I'm so clumsy.' After writing a chapter, such as now, I can either offer myself inner congratulations or tell myself I could do better, I am not as good a writer as others and so on. Much of this happens without us noticing, so becoming more aware of it, and giving ourselves a more positive internal message, can be very helpful.

It is important, if our insecurities are impacting us, to look at our support structures: such as mentoring if the issues are in a work situation, or from friends if the area of our insecurity is more personal. If the insecurity is seriously debilitating, affecting our mental health or disrupting relationships, then it can be very important to seek professional help. Insecurity is different from anxiety or panic attacks[10] but if it becomes serious enough to result in these, or other things which are affecting everyday life, then finding help is crucial.

As Christians, we are not immune from insecurity any more than we are from any other human vulnerability. The Bible is honest in its portrayal of humanity with all its frailties. In Exodus 3 and 4 the call of Moses to return to Egypt (from which he has fled having killed a slave driver) is described. Moses clearly feels inadequate for the task, despite God speaking to him directly in a number of ways. Eventually Moses admits what is perhaps one of the sources of his reluctance:[11] 'Pardon your servant, Lord. I have never been eloquent, neither in the past nor since you have spoken to your servant. I am slow of speech and tongue.'[12] God does not agree with his assessment but still supplies him help in the form of his brother,

Aaron, although the subsequent events suggest perhaps Moses' insecurities were unfounded. Gideon, called by God to take on the Midianites who were constantly plundering the Israelites, responds by saying 'but how can I save Israel? My clan is the weakest in Manasseh, and I am the least in my family.'[13] Yet both these people were able to overcome their feelings and fulfil their calling.

People of faith can be unhelpful in this area by placing unsupportive or even judgemental expectations on each other: such as responding to someone in distress by saying, 'You are not trusting in God enough.' Yet faith communities can also be helpful. Those in the church who are honest about their vulnerabilities, including their insecurities, yet either overcome them or persist despite them, model something healthy. The encouragement to try things out within the Christian community and have our efforts affirmed, even with their imperfections, can be confidence building. An environment in which people are valued and loved can help to offset other undermining messages from the past or present.

There are some aspects of biblical teaching that may be helpful in addressing our insecurities. The biblical writers, who lived in very uncertain times in a number of ways, have a great deal to say about God's provision. The psalmist declares 'The lions may grow weak and hungry, but those who seek the LORD lack no good thing',[14] and Jesus encourages his listeners to trust in God: 'And why do you worry about clothes? See how the flowers of the field grow. They do not labour or spin. Yet I tell you that not even Solomon in all his splendour was dressed like one of these. If that is how God clothes the grass of the field, which is here today and tomorrow is thrown into the fire, will he not much more clothe you – you of little faith?'[15] More generally, the Bible speaks of God's delight in us: 'The LORD your God is with you, the Mighty Warrior who saves. He will take great delight in you'[16] and of the love he has 'lavished on us' as his children.[17] Paul in his letters speaks of our adoption as children of God.[18] Adoption in the context Paul was writing about was highly significant. A natural-born child could be disowned, but an adopted child could not. All previous debts were erased, and for adopted children, inheritance did not just relate to something at death, but indicated that they shared fully everything the father possessed in the present, which gives an added meaning to being 'co-heirs with Christ'.[19] Reflecting on these promises and teaching can help to subvert the criticisms we receive, whether internally or externally.

One of the greatest areas of insecurity for us is the future, and in particular in relation to our limited mortality. Here the death and resurrection of Jesus offers us real hope. The words which are often used in funeral services were first spoken by Jesus himself, shortly before he raised Lazarus from the dead: 'I am the resurrection and the life. The one who believes in me will live, even though they die; and whoever lives by believing in me will never die.'[20] 1 Corinthians 15 spells out our reason for hope because of what Jesus has done, the path through death and resurrection he has taken before us and which enables him to accompany us on our own journeys through death.

The words of Romans 8 have given hope and a sense of security to many across the centuries, and so with those words I close this chapter:

> What, then, shall we say in response to these things? If God is for us, who can be against us? He who did not spare his own Son, but gave him up for us all – how will he not also, along with him, graciously give us all things? . . . No, in all these things we are more than conquerors through him who loved us. For I am convinced

that neither death nor life, neither angels nor demons, neither the present nor the future, nor any powers, neither height nor depth, nor anything else in all creation, will be able to separate us from the love of God that is in Christ Jesus our Lord.[21]

Reflection questions

- What are the things in your life, past or present, that have built in you a sense of security?
- Are there any areas in your life where you feel insecure?
- What might help you to build a greater sense of security in those areas?

Pilate: Surrender

'What is truth?' retorted Pilate.

John 18:38

The voice of Pilate

These tiresome people. Since Sejanus intervened with Tiberius, I have wondered more than once whether I was wise to accept the posting here. The usual ways I operate, sheer force of power and strength, seem to somehow bypass them. They simply will not give way.

There was that incident at Caesarea. What did they expect? They are under the control of Rome, of course they would see images of the emperor on our ensigns. But no, for reasons I am still not sure I understand, they were incensed, demonstrating at my headquarters and even my threat of death would not persuade them to desist. And now Sejanus' power is waning and with it, my protection. I pride myself on being a rational and practical man, yet the best way to manage them seems to elude me and the threat from Rome if I fail is constantly on my mind.

And now this Jesus. As procurator, of course, I had heard of him: it is my responsibility to root out and eliminate any threats and there have been so many power-seekers, gathering others around them, threatening the stability I need to maintain. I think nothing of eradicating would-be revolutionaries but my spies said he had preached love, supposedly healed some people and even, just in the previous few days, advocated the paying of our taxes. No threat, surely?

Then the religious leaders summoned me, making me go out to them because they said they could not sully themselves by entering my domain. I was not impressed. Even less so when they were vague with the charges and I could not understand why they could not deal with him themselves.

So, I brought him in to speak to me. Unlike the religious leaders he did not seem too proud to enter the palace of a Roman or feel he was dirtied by my presence. But I found him confusing, and the dialogue we entered into I still rehearse in the night when sleep eludes me, as it so often does. It was as if he and I were engaged in some kind of boxing match in which I was always wrong-footed. Exasperated, in the end all I could summon up was a weary, 'What is truth?' I have seen so much manoeuvering, so many lies and half-truths and sometimes I am sick of it all and long to lay down my responsibilities and find an outer and, even more difficult, an inner peace.

And then there was Procula, and this message about a dream. It is not like her to seek to interfere in matters related to the state and so I knew that she was genuinely troubled. As was I. Because, yes, he seemed innocent, and not just of the charges. There was something about him, as if, yes, he did not quite belong. I found him fascinating and unnerving in equal measure.

I hoped I had found a way out. Let Jesus go as a gift at their precious Passover time. Anything to keep the peace; the city is volatile enough at those festivals and Rome is constantly pressuring me to keep the Pax Romana. They do not want to send further troops to quell an uprising and it will be my posting – and my life – that are forfeited if I lose control.

But no, even that was denied me. They wanted some low-life rebel, who would probably cause me more trouble in the end, instead of this rabbi. Or maybe not, if Procula is right. And then I sensed the mood of the crowd change, and the ever-present threat of violence rose until I had no choice but to acquiesce.

So I called for a bowl, and washed my hands, declaring myself innocent. Yet even as I did so, uneasy to the very core of my being, I knew it was a futile gesture.

In the end, the truth was, I had surrendered.

John and Matthew's gospels tell part of his story:

Then the Jewish leaders took Jesus from Caiaphas to the palace of the Roman governor. By now it was early morning, and to avoid ceremonial uncleanness they did not enter the palace, because they wanted to be able to eat the Passover. So Pilate came out to them and asked, 'What charges are you bringing against this man?'

'If he were not a criminal,' they replied, 'we would not have handed him over to you.'

Pilate said, 'Take him yourselves and judge him by your own law.'

'But we have no right to execute anyone,' they objected. This took place to fulfil what Jesus had said about the kind of death he was going to die.

Pilate then went back inside the palace, summoned Jesus and asked him, 'Are you the king of the Jews?'

'Is that your own idea,' Jesus asked, 'or did others talk to you about me?'

'Am I a Jew?' Pilate replied. 'Your own people and chief priests handed you over to me. What is it you have done?'

Jesus said, 'My kingdom is not of this world. If it were, my servants would fight to prevent my arrest by the Jewish leaders. But now my kingdom is from another place.'

'You are a king, then!' said Pilate.

Jesus answered, 'You say that I am a king. In fact, the reason I was born and came into the world is to testify to the truth. Everyone on the side of truth listens to me.'

'What is truth?' retorted Pilate. With this he went out again to the Jews gathered there and said, 'I find no basis for a charge against him.' . . .

While Pilate was sitting on the judge's seat, his wife sent him this message: 'Don't have anything to do with that innocent man, for I have suffered a great deal today in a dream because of him.'

But the chief priests and the elders persuaded the crowd to ask for Barabbas and to have Jesus executed.

'Which of the two do you want me to release to you?' asked the governor.

'Barabbas,' they answered.

'What shall I do, then, with Jesus who is called the Messiah?' Pilate asked.

They all answered, 'Crucify him!'

'Why? What crime has he committed?' asked Pilate.

But they shouted all the louder, 'Crucify him!'

When Pilate saw that he was getting nowhere, but that instead an uproar was starting, he took water and washed his hands in front of the crowd. 'I am innocent of this man's blood,' he said. 'It is your responsibility!'

(John 18:28–38; Matt. 27:19–24)

Exploration of surrender

The week in which I was working on this chapter, Boris Johnson resigned as prime minister of the United Kingdom. Of his resignation statement outside number 10 Downing Street,[1] one commentator said 'It was not a resignation. It was a surrender.'[2]

At first sight, Pilate's behaviour, itself a surrender, seems inexplicable given what we know about him from other sources, including both Philo and Josephus. Pilate, who must have had some previous military experience, was the fifth governor of the area and is usually thought to have held the office between AD26 and 36/37, the main aims being to keep the peace, using force if necessary, and to ensure the trade route for corn from Egypt to Rome was kept open. He was responsible directly to Rome. Judea, together with Samaria and Idumaea, had originally become the responsibility of Archelaus on the death of his father, Herod the Great.[3] He was only 18, and ruled so harshly that the Jews themselves had asked for him to be replaced by a Roman procurator.

If Pilate was hoping for the posting to lead to better, or easier, things, he was destined to be disappointed – he was later recalled to Rome to be punished by Tiberius for the brutal and unnecessary massacre of a harmless group of Samaritans.[4] However, Tiberius died while Pilate was en route, and though there are various legends about what happened next, we do not know how his life ended.

Pilate was clearly capable of a stubborn disregard for the people he was ruling. Early in his posting he marched into Jerusalem, as was the practice of every governor, regular visits being one of the means of exercising control. Previous holders of the post had, before entering the city, removed the symbols of Rome from the standards in deference to the Jews' dislike of images.[5] Pilate refused, but was met with so much opposition he had to backtrack, the alternative being to arrest or kill every citizen. He was deeply unpopular for other reasons too: for example, on another occasion he built an aqueduct in the city, which would have been beneficial, but he used money from the temple funds.

Pilate was not afraid to use brutal means and would have no compunction in executing a troublemaker, so how are we to explain his apparent reluctance to execute one Jewish rabbi? Reading the biblical accounts, it is clear that Pilate was intrigued by Jesus, who must have presented so very differently from the aggressive, militant figures of the various Messianic claimants he had encountered. We sense that Pilate was struggling to understand this person brought before him, who to him seemed so enigmatic. Jesus seems willing to dialogue with him, even though he will not answer the charges brought against him.[6]

However fascinated he was by Jesus, Pilate's dilemma was real. Philo the Jewish writer describes that although capable of brutality, Pilate had a legitimate fear of being reported to the emperor and recalled to Rome which, as mentioned earlier, was later the case. The implied threat of the Jewish leaders' statement in John's account, 'If you let this man go, you are no friend of Caesar. Anyone who claims to be a king opposes Caesar'[7] was not an empty one. Other governors had been punished and if the emperor considered someone was no longer useful, they would send a message demanding the person kill themselves to save the soldiers the task.[8] 'Friend of Caesar' was an honorary title given to selected individuals and we know Pilate had been given it due to the intervention of Sejanus, an imperial official.[9] Any report of disloyalty and Pilate would lose his office, or even his life. There is a profound irony in the

declaration 'We have no king but Caesar'[10] given how deeply
Roman rule was hated by the Jewish people, but the threat to
Pilate was tangible.

Pilate washing his hands has become a familiar image in art
and literature and is thought by many sources to be the origin of the phrase 'I wash my hands of it/him/her'.[11] However
Psalm 26:6 does record the words, 'I wash my hands in inno-
cence, and go about your altar, Lord' which suggests an earlier
use of the practice as an expression of blamelessness.[12] It was
the custom of Jews to wash their hands on various occasions,[13]
and it appears Romans also did so, such as before offering temple sacrifices.[14] It is therefore not surprising that Pilate would
use this imagery to seek to absolve himself.

Ultimately, however, Pilate's actions remain an example of
surrendering to greater forces, which proved stronger than his
desire, for whatever reason, to free Jesus. What about our own
experiences of surrender?

To surrender can mean a number of things in different contexts. We speak of surrendering something in the sense of giving
it up: Pilate, of course, ultimately surrendered Jesus to death.[15]
We may speak of surrendering as handing someone over to the
authorities, or an object to the bank on repossession. However,
in the context of this chapter, I am looking at surrender as instances where we admit defeat, or give up a particular struggle.
We understand this meaning in a war situation, where we will
feel differently about that outcome depending on the side we
are on, but what about our everyday lives?

The word 'surrender', like patience, which we looked at
earlier in the chapter on Simeon, tends to be associated with
passivity or victimhood, as well as the failure and defeat we
think of in conflict situations. In some contexts, of course, it is
difficult and even dangerous to surrender, such as in a situation

where there is coercive control or abuse. At times the biblical teaching on marriages has been misused to teach that wives should surrender completely in marriage, even when there is abuse,[16] which is a clear misrepresentation of the Scriptures.

However, despite the risks of advocating the wrong kind of surrender, there are potentially more positive aspects to the concept. As we looked at in the chapter on power, from an early age we realise that ultimately, we are powerless in the face of some aspects of our lives, and to compensate for this we attempt to exercise various levels of control. In the recovery programmes such as Alcoholics Anonymous, Narcotics Anonymous, etc., the first step is to recognise that the individual is powerless over their addiction, and that as a result their life has become unmanageable. There is, as has sometimes been pointed out,[17] a choice of what to surrender to – the addiction or the recovery programme, a choice with a significant difference in potential outcome. The basis of the Twelve Steps reminds all of us that the first step in overwhelming situations may be what I call 'positive surrender': a letting go of our need to try to control things, or indeed people, opening the creative possibility of looking at the situation differently. I am reminded of the process of giving birth: I could have tried desperately and ultimately fruitlessly to control the progression of labour. Much better, in my experience, to surrender to the rhythms of my body, and where necessary to helpful interventions from the medics. To give another example, there is a sense in which I could try to continue to control the lives of my grown-up children, as I did when they were small, risking a fracture in relationship. Or I can surrender them and myself to their adult lives and decisions.

The third step in the recovery programmes mentioned above is 'a decision to turn our will and our lives over to the care of God as we understood Him'.[18] Most faiths, including Christianity, involve an element of surrender to the object of faith and worship. One of the first hymns I learned, as a new Christian from a non-Christian background, was 'All to Jesus I Surrender'.[19] I sang it enthusiastically but had little real understanding of what that meant and still, after some fifty years as a Christian, certainly do not fully practise it. It is a process.

The Bible does use the language of war and conflict, from the (sometimes very difficult to read) stories of literal battles in the Old Testament[20] to the language of spiritual struggle in the New.[21] The letter of James has an interesting reference to a mixture of surrender and resistance where James encourages the recipients of the letter to: 'Submit yourselves, then, to God. Resist the devil, and he will flee from you.'[22] Both surrender and opposition are part of the Christian journey.

The life of Jesus models both of these aspects. There are moments of resistance, such as when Peter implies that there is an easier way for Jesus than suffering and receives the rebuke, 'Get behind me, Satan! You are a stumbling-block to me; you do not have in mind the concerns of God, but merely human concerns.'[23] There is the implication in the words at the conclusion of the temptation story that the devil 'left him until an opportune time',[24] that this was an ongoing struggle for Jesus, seen not least in the agony of Gethsemane,[25] and the taunts of the onlookers at the cross: 'Let this Messiah, this king of Israel, come down now from the cross, that we may see and believe.'[26] For Jesus, a refusal to surrender to the easy way meant the lonely path to the cross. At the end, it meant surrendering into the loving, welcoming arms of the Father, task complete.[27]

To willingly surrender to anyone or anything requires trust. The biblical picture is of a loving and faithful God who is worthy of our confidence, as the psalmist asserts: 'Those who know your name trust in you, for you, LORD, have never for-saken those who seek you.'[28] We begin our journey of faith with an initial surrender to follow Jesus, to take up the cross of discipleship daily. As we continue, we choose to submit to God's work of transformation, including sometimes the pain-ful work of pruning by the Gardener.[29] And, when the time comes, we hope that rather than rage against the coming dark-ness, as Dylan Thomas urged his dying father,[30] we may, like Jesus, rest confident that the final journey is into Love.

Perhaps ultimately the question is not whether we will sur-render, but when, and to what or whom, we do so.

Reflection questions

- What does the word 'surrender' mean to you?
- Which are the areas of your life you find easy, and dif-ficult, to surrender?
- Is there anything which you are being called to surren-der, or surrender to, at this time in your life?

Thomas: Honesty

*Unless I see the nail marks in his hands and put
my finger where the nails were, and put my hand
into his side, I will not believe.*

John 20:25

The voice of Thomas

I could not believe it. And that was the whole problem. I
wanted to, how I wanted to. But I just couldn't. Because he
was dead. And dead people do not come back to life.

It is hard to describe the horror of the days that preceded
those extraordinary, life-changing events. Three years we had
spent with him, three amazing years. He was like no one else
I had ever met, and though we were in many ways a strange
group, I enjoyed the camaraderie, the sense of being part of
something really important. I did not always understand Jesus:
all of us struggled at times and it was usually me who said so.
My mother always said I was too honest for my own good, but
it is just me. I don't know how to be any other way. Peter and I
always got on well in that way. Both of us unafraid to speak out.

But I loved Jesus, I really loved him. There was a point
when we could sense the clouds gathering around us. Jesus

kept talking about dying, but it was more than that. The rest thought we should go back north, but Jesus had his mind set on Jerusalem, I could tell that, and I was ready to go and die with him, and said so to the others.

Except I wasn't ready, not in the end. After that strange meal, where I struggled again to understand both Jesus' actions and his words, we headed to Gethsemane. Jesus loved it there. I think the quiet helped him pray, though he never seemed to find that hard. I do. Very hard. Sometimes the words seem so empty.

It seemed he needed the space, and left eight of us sitting under a tree before going to find a quiet corner. He had taken Peter, James and John with him, as he often did, but I gathered later he had left even them and gone on further to be completely alone. The three of them always found it hard to talk about it afterwards. They would only say Jesus was in agony, and then shake their heads. Looking back, I could see why Jesus was frightened, if he could sense even a little of what lay ahead.

It was so quiet there, and we chatted for a while, trying to understand what Jesus had been saying at the meal, and then I dozed, until Matthew nudged me awake. He had seen the light of torches through the trees and just as we roused the others, Jesus and the other three rejoined us. To my shock, I realised that Judas was at the head of a crowd coming towards us. I had wondered where he had gone but never expected to see him there. He went up to Jesus and kissed him. I was bewildered. What was he doing? A moment later, I realised in horror as Jesus was arrested – he had led them to Jesus. What on earth was he thinking? Why?

There was uproar. We were shouting at the men, yelling that Jesus was innocent, screaming at them to let him go. Peter was raging, swinging his sword, and he injured someone – we later found out it was the high priest's servant. For a second, we froze and fell silent, thinking we would all be arrested. Jesus spoke up, healed the man, and told us to stop, that as he had told us, this was to fulfil the Scripture. I knew he had said that, many times. But really, this? He called something similar to the crowd.

I'm ashamed to say the next bit, but I must. I ran. All through Yom Shishi[1] and Shabbat I hid myself in the Passover crowds. I was ashamed that I had let him down, and heartbroken. I pretended to be a late arrival to the festival and asked around what had happened. They had killed him. My Jesus was dead. I wept and raged, curling up like a child in dark corners where I couldn't be seen. I could not share my pain with anyone, not even the other disciples. I had no strength to support them in their distress. I just wanted to be alone.

Eventually on Yom Rishon[2] I crept back to the disciples, expecting to find them as broken as I was. Yet instead, I had an enormous shock. Instead of grief-stricken, they were radiant, beside themselves with joy. For a moment I thought the sorrow had driven them mad. Then, as I listened to them, I thought it really had. They had seen Jesus, they said. They surrounded me, as if that encircling would somehow make me believe it. I looked from one face to another, eager as children, and I hated to crush them, but I could not pretend to feel something I simply didn't. He was dead, and we needed to accept that. 'I'm not believing you unless I see for myself,' I said, 'unless I touch him.' I could see they were disappointed, but what else could I say? It was the truth.

And then, he came.

John's gospel tells part of his story:

> Now Thomas (also known as Didymus), one of the Twelve, was
> not with the disciples when Jesus came. So the other disciples told
> him, 'We have seen the Lord!'
>
> But he said to them, 'Unless I see the nail marks in his hands
> and put my finger where the nails were, and put my hand into his
> side, I will not believe.'
>
> A week later his disciples were in the house again, and Thomas
> was with them. Though the doors were locked, Jesus came and
> stood among them and said, 'Peace be with you!' Then he said
> to Thomas, 'Put your finger here; see my hands. Reach out your
> hand and put it into my side. Stop doubting and believe.'
>
> Thomas said to him, 'My Lord and my God!'
>
> Then Jesus told him, 'Because you have seen me, you have be-
> lieved; blessed are those who have not seen and yet have believed.'
>
> (John 20:24–29)

Exploration of honesty

For a long time I have been intrigued by the character of
Thomas, mainly known for this encounter with Jesus after
Jesus' resurrection. Some people call him Doubting Thomas,
of course, but this enrages me on so many levels. I'm glad the
Bible only refers to him as 'the twin'.[3]

As you will gather from this chapter so far, for me Thomas
is associated much more with honesty. I suspect that what is
happening for Thomas at this point in the story is much more
about the searing pain of loss and a destructive sense of isolation. For reasons on which we can only speculate, but which I
suspect owes much to a broken-hearted need for psychic space,

Thomas was missing on the first Easter Day. Like the Little Match Girl in Hans Christian Andersen's story, he is at risk of dying in the cold while others celebrate.[4] He's on the edge of the group, always a profoundly unnerving and isolating place to be. Exposed and insular, he is only asking to experience the same encounter as the others: to be like them, to be one of them again.

In contrast to the implied criticism of his nickname, Thomas is displaying an integrity which is applauded biblically. We particularly see this in the Psalms, the Hebrew worship book which contains a raw honesty found less in our sometimes overly individualistic and triumphant worship today.[5] Thomas won't sacrifice his truthfulness just to avoid rejection: though it says much of the other disciples that they clearly continue to see him as one of the group, and their dogged acceptance of him is what ensures him being with them when Jesus appears to them again.

Thomas wanted the evidence of his eyes before he could believe that Jesus had been resurrected. He was an honest realist, requiring proof before he risked his heart again, fragile and vulnerable as it was after the trauma of recent days. This says surely more about his humanity than his ability or otherwise to believe.

It is a gift from Thomas' honesty that it led to a blessing for us, in our time, in the words of Jesus: 'Because you have seen me, you have believed; blessed are those who have not seen and yet have believed.'[6] These words have comforted many since who, unlike Thomas, were unable to see Jesus physically resurrected.

There are many ways in which we may think of honesty.[7] In this chapter I want to look briefly at one, and then concentrate on the type of honesty shown by Thomas. The first is what I have called practical honesty: the kind expressed in what we

say and do, or don't do; for example, not stealing, lying, breaking promises or misleading others by our words or actions.
Interestingly, there is more research on dishonesty than honesty. It is surprising that there appear to be only two academic
philosophical studies on the topic in the past half century.[8]
One fascinating study using an honesty box found that people
were more honest when there were eyes 'watching' them, even
though the eyes were only a photograph.[9] The theory is that
honesty is needed for a society to work well: so we are inclined
to selfish behaviour when acting alone and unseen, but when
we think we are being watched we behave more cooperatively
and generously in the hope of receiving the same in return.
This is so instinctive that it seems even a photograph steers us
to behave in that way.

Clearly this kind of practical honesty is important biblically.
Several of the commandments centre on the issue: 'You shall
not commit adultery' (honesty in promise-keeping), 'You shall
not steal' (financial honesty) and 'You shall not give false testimony against your neighbour' (honesty in speech).[10] Paul
writes of the necessity of putting off falsehood in his instructions on Christian living.[11] Earlier in the same chapter, he uses
the oft-quoted phrase 'speaking the truth in love'.[12] While this
is often used of personal conversation (and sometimes misused to justify rudeness), the context is actually of teaching
in the church. However, the principle of the primacy of love,
expressed elsewhere, particularly in 1 Corinthians 13, is important.[13] It is possible to be honest but from motives of cruelty or
self-service: technically honest but morally lacking.

Research suggests that most people consider themselves honest even though at times they lie. Most lies are self-centred: to
protect our own interests in some way, such as lying about our
availability to avoid something we don't want to do or, more

seriously, lying to avoid detection in a crime or moral lapse. Sometimes choices around honesty are complex. For example, there may be occasions when we can see something in another person or situation which we can choose either to point out, or not. At times the loving thing may be to say nothing: what a previous boss of mine once referred to as a 'pastoral silence'. This may be temporary, awaiting a moment when someone is less tired, for example, or may result in a long-standing silence on an issue. At other times, the loving thing is to speak out. Great discernment is needed to tell the difference, especially when we are motivated by care for others: such as the friend who raves about a new dress they are wearing and asks our opinion when we don't think it suits them. In instances such as those, the repercussions are relatively trivial. It is debateable whether the temporary difficulty of speaking the truth might still be better, to enable a longer-term trust that we will always speak the truth. Speaking the truth about a potential character defect or worrying course of action, though a difficult conversation, also gives the other person the opportunity to change. There is, of course, the caveat that we will always be speaking the truth as we see it, with an inevitable subjective element. In other instances, such as hiding families in wartime, the lie may be lifesaving, where arguably the command to honesty is superseded by a higher moral principle. In reality these occasions are very rare.

The second aspect of honesty, which I want to concentrate on, is what I might term 'emotional honesty': being prepared to express what we truly think and feel. Thomas displayed this: he knew he was not able to believe and was able to say so even though there must have been subtle pressure to pretend to believe in order to be accepted by the group. There are at least two stages to emotional honesty. The first is we actually need to *know* what it is that we do feel. That is not always as easy as it seems. Sometimes we somatise: our body reacts in a way which may be emotional in origin, and we are aware of the physical symptoms but not the root. This was one of the backgrounds to Freud's work: he explored what he called 'conversion hysteria', where an underlying anxiety presents in a physical symptom, in his case patients with partial paralysis. It is important to say, of course, that not all physical symptoms have an emotional root and they should always be checked by a doctor if worrying. However, we can recognise the reality of the two-way link between our bodies and emotions: when nervous we can experience digestive disturbance, for example,[14] and our immune system can become compromised in times of stress or grief.[15] We can have a sense of unease, physically or in other ways, but have difficulty pinpointing what the root cause is, particularly if it is an emotion we are uncomfortable with, such as anger or grief. So, we may experience anger, for example, as a headache, rather than being able to recognise what it is.

Another difficulty is that we may know there is a thought or emotion lurking inside but we do not know what it is so cannot name it. One of the best gifts we can give small children is to help them give their emotions a name. It will help the feeling to be less frightening and open the way for them to be able to share their emotions in the future. We can, in contrast, also use language to minimise an emotion. When counselling, if I tentatively suggested someone might be angry (sometimes sensing they were actually livid) they would often say something like 'No. I'm not angry, I'm just cross.' So, the first step, which is an ongoing journey for most of us, is to become self-aware enough to access and name the emotions we are experiencing.

The second step is to be willing, when appropriate, to share those emotions with others. Here emotional honesty may be the opposite not of dishonesty, but of silence. This is not straightforward and there are two ends of the spectrum which are potential traps for us. The first is to be so open that we share everything with everyone, with no filter to either protect ourselves or recognise the impact on the other person. We can share at an inappropriate time or with an inappropriate person, for example, someone who cannot hold a confidence or helpfully listen. The other end of the spectrum is to be closed emotionally to others out of self-protection and not share our feelings. This is perhaps more the case for many of us, certainly it is for me, with the attendant risk that when we do find someone we trust, we emotionally haemorrhage and later experience feelings of extreme vulnerability. We will look at the topic of vulnerability in the final chapter.

This kind of honesty can be particularly challenging for church leaders. Yesterday I was in conversation with someone with responsibility in a church who was expressing how difficult it can be to express pain, anger, or doubt. There is an expectation that those of us with such roles are somehow different, having a level of holiness which puts us above such things. This is wrong on two levels. In the first place we are not any different from anyone else. We do experience those things as much as others and need safe spaces to air them. I have been grateful for spiritual directors over the years who have enabled exactly that, and I am encouraged by the rise in numbers of those in caring roles, including ministry, seeking pastoral supervision.[16] It is important, without our pastoral work or preaching becoming personal therapy, to subvert the notion of our difference with our own honesty. The second way in which this idea is wrong is that to not experience those things would make us less able to draw alongside those in our church families who do, with empathy and sensitivity. The Bible is honest about the range of human emotions, and makes it clear that Jesus experienced them too, needing companionship in the darkest of times. We see this in his poignant words in Gethsemane to the sleeping disciples: 'Couldn't you men keep watch with me for one hour?'[17]

Our honesty with others, costly though it may be to us, can open us to the companionship of others in our own dark times. Stripped of the pride which sometimes isolates us in our false independence, in our vulnerability as we express our fears, grief or doubt we can experience a depth of relationship not possible in our self-sufficiency. Helen Keller, who was both blind and deaf, spoke of the way in which walking with a friend in the dark was better than walking alone in the light. What we may also do is open the door to others, experiencing in us an emotional honesty which may free them to be able to do the same.

Reflection questions

- Are there any areas of your life where you find it easier to be honest than others?
- How easy do you find it to be honest about your emotions with others?
- How comfortable are you when others are emotionally honest with you?

Stephen: Forgiveness

Then he fell on his knees and cried out, 'Lord,
do not hold this sin against them.' When he had
said this, he fell asleep.

Acts 7:60

The voice of Stephen

It won't be long now. They have such fury in their eyes, such vitriol written across all of their faces. They have hauled me outside the city, as our law requires. In their minds, they are justified. I am inciting others to worship a false God. A few months ago, before I met Jesus, perhaps I would have felt the same. I always loved being one of God's people, and treasured our Law.

But once Jesus found me, it was a different story. I still love God, and our Law, but I discovered such grace, realising that his love was not about what I did for him, but what he had already done for me. As a result, I was happy to serve him in any way I could. It was an honour to be chosen and I loved being part of the distribution of food, part of God providing for his people now, as once he had in the desert. Each time I was handing it out, I remembered the story Peter had told me about Jesus multiplying the food, and prayed that the same thing might be true for us so that all those in need could be fed. And God blessed us in so many ways, working wonders, bringing people to new life.

Yet in others I began to sense a change in atmosphere. The questions were more hostile and less interested. People responded so differently to our Good News. Some were thrilled to receive Jesus and to follow him, joining our growing numbers. Yet for others, it seemed as though talk of Jesus released a deep anger in them. Their hearts were closed. They were afraid to accept Jesus as *mashiach*,[1] sensing that it meant changing completely, which yes, it does. What they could not see was the freedom that it brought, that God was, after what seemed such a long silence, working in a new way.

Peter had spoken to me about when he was before the Sanhedrin. For them it was Gamaliel who had turned things around. Perhaps more importantly, he also told me about the words of Jesus: the warning that we would find ourselves before the authorities, but that we should not fear, because his Spirit would give us the words to say. I tried to hold on to that as the accusation of blasphemy was brought and they took me, too, in front of the Sanhedrin. I remembered that Jesus had faced them first and prayed that he would help me as he had promised, that his love would shine through me.

And yes, that is what happened. Somewhere from deep within me words flowed, as if I was travelling through the history of our people, tracing God at work and the ways in which all of us as God's people had failed to see it and, even worse, had obstructed so much of God's purposes and even persecuted those who spoke for him. I knew that somehow God was there, speaking through me. Then, as the words ceased, in a wonderful moment I could somehow see beyond, see Jesus, and so, oblivious to how they would respond, I simply spoke out the beauty I could see.

They could not understand. For me there will be no Gamaliel to speak up. I would have hoped to have had longer to share the Good News, but I have to trust God that somehow this will be in his purposes. I scan the crowd of angry faces, and a young man at whose feet they have laid their coats, standing and watching. Lord, somehow use this for your glory.

The stones are beginning to come, and the pain is intense. I endeavour, through the growing agony, to gasp what I know will be a last prayer. I try to remember what I have heard from the apostles about Jesus' last moments, his final prayers, and to echo those. 'Jesus, I'm yours, please take me home.' And, with one last look at them all, 'Please forgive them.'

I'm ready, Jesus. I am coming to you. *Hineni.*[2] Here I am.

The book of Acts tells part of his story:

In those days when the number of disciples was increasing, the Hellenistic Jews among them complained against the Hebraic Jews because their widows were being overlooked in the daily distribution of food. So the Twelve gathered all the disciples together and said, 'It would not be right for us to neglect the ministry of the word of God in order to wait on tables. Brothers and sisters, choose seven men from among you who are known to be full of the Spirit and wisdom. We will turn this responsibility over to them and will give our attention to prayer and the ministry of the word.'

This proposal pleased the whole group. They chose Stephen, a man full of faith and of the Holy Spirit; also Philip, Procorus, Nicanor, Timon, Parmenas, and Nicolas from Antioch, a convert to Judaism. They presented these men to the apostles, who prayed and laid their hands on them.

So the word of God spread. The number of disciples in Jerusalem increased rapidly, and a large number of priests became obedient to the faith.

Now Stephen, a man full of God's grace and power, performed great wonders and signs among the people. Opposition arose, however, from members of the Synagogue of the Freedmen (as it was called) – Jews of Cyrene and Alexandria as well as the provinces of Cilicia and Asia – who began to argue with Stephen. But they could not stand up against the wisdom the Spirit gave him as he spoke.

Then they secretly persuaded some men to say, 'We have heard Stephen speak blasphemous words against Moses and against God.'

So they stirred up the people and the elders and the teachers of the law. They seized Stephen and brought him before the Sanhedrin. They produced false witnesses, who testified, 'This fellow never stops speaking against this holy place and against the law. For we have heard him say that this Jesus of Nazareth will destroy this place and change the customs Moses handed down to us.'

All who were sitting in the Sanhedrin looked intently at Stephen, and they saw that his face was like the face of an angel.

(Acts 6:1–15)

The next section describes how Stephen spoke to the Sanhedrin:

When the members of the Sanhedrin heard this, they were furious and gnashed their teeth at him. But Stephen, full of the Holy Spirit, looked up to heaven and saw the glory of God, and Jesus standing at the right hand of God. 'Look,' he said, 'I see heaven open and the Son of Man standing at the right hand of God.'

At this they covered their ears and, yelling at the top of their voices, they all rushed at him, dragged him out of the city and began to stone him. Meanwhile, the witnesses laid their coats at the feet of a young man named Saul.

While they were stoning him, Stephen prayed, 'Lord Jesus, receive my spirit.' Then he fell on his knees and cried out, 'Lord, do not hold this sin against them.' When he had said this, he fell asleep.

(Acts 7:54–60)

Exploration of forgiveness

I do need to start this section with a caveat. The topic of forgiveness, a voluntary choosing to let go of our anger, bitterness and desire for retribution for a wrong, is huge. Inevitably, therefore, I will only be able to say a very few things on what is perhaps one of the biggest challenges we face not just as individuals, the area on which I am concentrating, but also as societies. It is, in addition, an area of the greatest sensitivity. Some of you who read these words will have been on the receiving end of terrible wrongs which have left you deeply scarred and have impacted on every area of your life.[3] Please do not hear anything I say as implying forgiveness is easy. It is not and, if we are able to offer it, can be very costly. There will be some for whom it is a lifelong journey, others for whom simply to begin to be willing to forgive is a huge step and may be as far as it is possible to go, at least for now. All I can do here is offer a few words which I pray may be helpful.

The other note of caution is that forgiveness does not necessarily mean that a restoration in relationship is possible or even wise. Lewis Smedes has written what is now a classic book *Forgive and Forget*. The title I think is unhelpful, taken, of course, from the common phrase, because in reality, if a hurt is deep, we do not forget, and arguably should not do so. In fact, he says exactly that in the book.[4] He writes about four stages of forgiving: hurting (which may entail allowing ourselves to feel pain we have buried), hating (allowing the anger space) and healing (which includes learning to see the person who has hurt us in a new light, what he calls 'magic eyes'). The fourth stage he sees as coming together: inviting the person back into our lives, which may or may not be taken up by the other. This stage I think may be appropriate for some situations.[5] However, in others, such as where there has been violence or abuse, it may not be. In those instances, it is an internal journey towards forgiveness, without restoration of relationship, that is the right way forward. This comment aside, there is much that is very helpful in Smedes' book on this very difficult subject.

Unlike some of the other topics in this book, there has been considerable interest from researchers in the area of forgiveness, with some interesting results. Luskin's[6] significant work, which contributed to both the American Forgiveness Project and the work of the Northern Irish HOPE project, found that practising forgiveness led to an increase in both physical and mental/ emotional well-being.[7] These findings have been borne out in a number of other studies.[8]

Psychologist Shauna Shapiro[9] describes five skills which can help us in this difficult area. The first is acceptance that something traumatic or hurtful has happened, and that it cannot be changed. This stage may come about unexpectedly when memories resurface, which can happen for many reasons: for example, when our own children (if we have them) reach the age that we were when an event or series of events took place. If the incident is recent, sometimes we are initially shocked and it can take a while to process the reality of what has happened.

The second skill, she suggests, is emotional regulation: recognising and naming the impact on us and then seeking to purposefully calm our response. This is not always as easy as it sounds. Many of us minimise the hurt we have experienced in the hope of lessening its effect, but in fact what that more often does is simply drive it underground, where it tends to quietly fester like an unseen infection which finally overcomes us. To recognise our feelings and use words of the right strength is important: which may mean saying 'I am devastated' rather than 'that stung me'. In my early years, as I indicated in my last book *Held in Your Bottle*,[10] I constantly received the message 'Don't make a fuss'. I suspect it was not my parents' intention, but it meant for many years I minimised the painful experiences of those years and it was not until much later that I was able to find the words to fit. As I said in the chapter on honesty, giving children a vocabulary for their emotions, including their hurts, is very important.

In forgiveness, it may be particularly important to recognise our anger. Anger goes with pain: if you stub your toe badly, you may yelp or cry, or utter a few choice expletives. Anger is therefore the flip side of pain, but so often people, especially Christians, suppress anger or call it something else. Anger is an understandable, even at times justified, response, but we will need to deal with it in the long run: neither denying it nor nursing it are helpful. The third skill is shifting perspectives – what psychologists call reframing,[11] stepping back from the messages we give ourselves and the narrative we make of our lives and looking at them differently, finding a broader or different perspective. The fourth is empathy and compassion. When I began to understand some of the ways in which my upbringing had impacted me negatively (however well-meaning my parents were), it helped me to realise the difficulties they had themselves encountered. It is very important to say at this point that empathy for another does not mean that their actions are excused. The fact that something needs forgiving means by definition that it was wrong. But we are all flawed and damaged human beings: as someone once said to me, 'Hurt people hurt people.' The final skill Shapiro outlines is radical responsibility: owning our own responses, monitoring, and if necessary, changing, our own behaviour. No one else can make the journey of forgiveness for us: it is ours to take.

The research which has been conducted into forgiveness has had different emphases, but all of it has highlighted three things: the need for a realistic view of the offence (which may mean seeing it either as less or more significant or severe than we first thought), the need to try to exercise empathy, and finally relinquishing our right to punish the offender. This latter point does not, of course, necessarily negate the need for the law to take its course when it has been broken in some way. Forgiveness, as I said earlier, is not to condone or excuse what happened, and it does not necessarily free a person from the consequences of their actions.[12]

While forgiveness may be easier if the other person takes responsibility for their actions, it is not a prerequisite. Often, we need to forgive someone who is either unaware they have hurt us, or do not care that they have. They may not even still be alive to find out the impact they have had on us, or may be people we do not know, for example, if we were abandoned by a parent we never met. None of these things mean forgiveness cannot take place.

Forgiving ourselves can be as difficult, if not more so, than forgiving others, especially when we cannot rectify what happened. In the process of writing my second book, I made a mistake with the details of one of the endorsers, which I did not realise until the book was printed. Immediately I apologised, but the person concerned sensed I was finding it difficult and encouraged me to forgive myself. I recognise that I am my own harshest critic and can find it hard to forgive myself small mistakes as well as larger ones, in particular if I feel I have hurt others. It can be important, if we struggle in this area, to avoid globalising what we have done: 'I'm always doing this . . .' It is all too easy for our view of ourselves to become skewed so that we fail to see the good aspects of ourselves and the loving choices we have made. Jesus' command to 'Love your neighbour as yourself'[13] assumes that we will indeed love ourselves. This is for many of us a challenge, particularly if we have been on the receiving end of a lot of negative messages, which may be one of the very things we need to forgive others for.

There are some extraordinary, indeed inspiring, stories of forgiveness in the most extreme of circumstances,[14] but I have chosen not to look at any of them in this chapter. The main reason for this is in their very extremity they can feel alien to us. One response is to wonder if we would ever find the strength in similar circumstances, the reality being that we will never know unless we find ourselves in them: we can rehearse how we would like to respond, or worry about how we might, but actually can never tell ahead of time. The other reason is that these dramatic and tragic examples can blunt us to the realisation that there are many smaller instances where we need to practise forgiveness: such as when someone ignores us, makes an offhand comment, or forgets something important to us. R.T. Kendall points out that giving forgiveness needs to be a daily discipline,[15] and if we practise it on the smaller slights, it will grow our capacity to be forgiving for the deeper hurts. Although there is some evidence that the ability to forgive may be linked to personality traits,[16] it is primarily an act of will, which may or may not be accompanied with feelings, and one which will need to be repeated, perhaps frequently, as the hurt or damage resurfaces.

Forgiveness is at the heart of the gospel and a major biblical theme. In the Old Testament, God's willingness to forgive is highlighted, including in the Psalms: '[God] will not always accuse, nor will he harbour his anger for ever; he does not treat us as our sins deserve or repay us according to our iniquities. For as high as the heavens are above the earth, so great is his love for those who fear him; as far as the east is from the west, so far has he removed our transgressions from us.'[17] Provision was made in the sacrificial system for people to experience that forgiveness[18] and the prophet Jeremiah declared that it would be at the heart of the new covenant God had promised: 'No longer will they teach their neighbour, or say to one another, "Know the LORD," because they will all know me, from the least of them to the greatest," declares the LORD. "For I will forgive their wickedness and will remember their sins no more."'[19] God is clearly portrayed as a God who forgives. This is supremely demonstrated in the death of Jesus for us, making a way so that 'if we confess our sins, he is faithful and just and will forgive us our sins and purify us from all unrighteousness'.[20] This receiving of forgiveness, which we all need,[21] paves the way for the forgiveness that we need to offer to others. *The Message* expresses it in this way: 'If we claim that we're free of sin, we're only fooling ourselves. A claim like that is errant nonsense. On the other hand, if we admit our sins – simply come clean about them – he won't let us down; he'll be true to himself. He'll forgive our sins and purge us of all wrongdoing.'[22]

Within the teaching of Jesus forgiveness was, unsurprisingly, a significant theme. The Lord's prayer, a pattern for prayer in response to the disciples' request for Jesus to teach them to pray, includes in Luke's version the words, 'Forgive us our sins, for we also forgive everyone who sins against us.'[23] After the equivalent prayer in Matthew, contained in the Sermon on the Mount, Jesus is recorded as adding the words: 'For if you forgive other people when they sin against you, your heavenly Father will also forgive you. But if you do not forgive others their sins, your Father will not forgive your sins.'[24]

Peter clearly recognised the challenge which forgiving others poses and so sought to give it a manageable limit: 'Lord, how many times shall I forgive my brother or sister who sins against me? Up to seven times?'[25] He probably thought he was being generous, as the rabbis suggested three. Jesus' reply set a totally different standard, variously translated at seventy-seven or seventy times seven: in other words, without number, constantly. This, I suspect, represents both forgiving once for numerous single hurts, and forgiving repeatedly the same hurt where it is deep and has ongoing repercussions. The Greek word used in the Bible for forgiving is literally 'letting go': the task for us is to open our hands and let go of the anger and resentment which we so easily, and sometimes very understandably, can experience when we have been wronged. Love, in contrast, 'keeps no record of wrongs'.[26]

In response to Peter's question, Jesus told the parable of the unforgiving (or unmerciful) servant,[27] where the servant is forgiven a huge debt, which he could never have repaid, yet refuses to show mercy to his fellow servant over a tiny one, and as a result of his harshness suffers the wrath of the master. Jesus concludes this sobering parable with the words: 'This is how my heavenly Father will treat each of you unless you forgive your brother or sister from your heart.'[28] Jesus made it clear that an attitude of forgiveness is important in both prayer and worship.[29] It is, of course, something he himself practised even in his final moments, as our supreme example: 'Father, forgive them, for they do not know what they are doing.'[30]

Paul, who having witnessed Stephen's death must surely have had his last words etched in his memory, taught frequently in his letters about the importance of forgiving one another in the church community. Wherever people gather together, there will be hurts and upsets. Paul clearly valued unity within the church,[31] and the holding of grudges and resentments quickly undermines that. The forgiveness he urged was based first of all on the forgiveness that we have received: 'Bear with each other and forgive one another if any of you has a grievance against someone. Forgive as the Lord forgave you.'[32] It helps, I find, when dealing with hurts within the church family to reflect on the fact that we all stand as equals at the foot of the cross, equally in need of forgiveness.

This persistent link between giving and receiving forgiveness in the biblical teaching undoubtedly presents a challenge for us. N.T. Wright writes that we can sometimes hold a false image of God as like a kindly grandfather who will not give a gift to a sulky child who refuses to give to anyone else. Rather, he says, forgiveness must be more like the air in our lungs, both breathed in and breathed out.[33] Resentments fracture relationships in church communities and can have a devastating effect on both fellowship and witness. John and Carol Arnott in their teaching talk about the river of God's grace: when we hold on to a grudge, we take ourselves out of that river. Standing in it, we are able to both give and receive forgiveness.[34] We cannot escape the teaching of the Bible, but we also, if we are to practise it, need to be honest about how difficult it can be and, where we need to, receive help to work things through to help us put it into practice. Sometimes, the first step is asking God to help us to be willing, to pave the way for what Lewis Smedes calls an unseen miracle.[35]

We know very little about Stephen, and nothing about either his family or how he came to faith. All we have are the few verses in Acts, and his place in history as the first, though sadly far from the last, Christian martyr. I have always been struck, however, by the small difference between his words of forgiveness and those of Jesus from the cross.[36] Jesus prays forgiveness because those crucifying him do not know what they are doing: they have no idea of the unique nature of the person they are crucifying or the enormity of it. To those nailing him to the cross, Jesus is just another law-breaker. Stephen simply prays forgiveness: they *do* know what they are doing: they are stoning another person, another Jew like them. Our own forgiveness can be one of either kind: sometimes given to those who do not know that they have hurt us, or the extent of it. At other times, people are all too well aware. Forgiveness is a challenge either way: but it is one, if we want to be Christ-like, which we do at the very least need to be prepared to begin to undertake, offering ourselves the same compassion we try to gift others, as we travel its complex, and often long, road.

Reflection questions

- How easy do you find it to forgive the small hurts received from others?
- Is there a particularly difficult journey of forgiveness God is asking you to make? Are there resources or people who might be able to help with the next step?
- Is forgiving yourself challenging or easy for you? What difference might it make knowing God has forgiven you?

20

Paul: Vulnerability

> *Three times I pleaded with the Lord to take it*
> *away from me. But he said to me, 'My grace is*
> *sufficient for you, for my power is made perfect*
> *in weakness.'*
>
> 2 Cor. 12:8–9

The voice of Paul

When, God? When is this crippling pain going to end?

Sometimes I feel that the burden you have placed on me is too heavy. It is as if my life and work for you is an overloaded vessel that is starting to take in water: I am frantically trying to bail it out but I am losing, and am so afraid that everything will be wasted and I will have failed.

I wanted to feel invincible, that anything was possible. And so much has been. The responses to the preaching, the miracles. Churches being planted, places where the truth about Jesus can be preached and lives can be transformed. At times I felt like a colossus for you, striding across your world, as though together we could do anything. I wanted to feel strong, invulnerable.

But that time in Ephesus, and all it brought, nearly destroyed me. It was as if everything was conspiring against me. The time in prison, not just the physical isolation but the sense that I could not be doing what you asked of me. Always so much criticism. And the worry for the church at Corinth. You know, God, my fear that crippled me, that I had made things worse with that letter, when my heart had been to help, to mend the rift between them and me.

And now this pain, God. It is too much. It twists and grips me, waking me at night and haunting me by day. It is all I can think about, it blinds me. I know that you can heal me. I have seen you heal others. And I have prayed, begged, wept. I have felt a failure, because somehow my prayers have not yielded the results I craved. I have felt angry with you, when I know for you to relieve me of my suffering would be so easy. I have cried out to you like the psalmists of old. I have been bewildered: surely you do not want our mission to be curtailed when there is still so much need for your gospel to be heard. Your world is so broken.

Why, God?

Yet now, in the silence, as all my prayers and protests are spent and my tears flow, I hear your gentle voice. 'Let go. Stop trying to be strong and let me be strong in you. I am enough.'

2 Corinthians tells part of his story:

I must go on boasting. Although there is nothing to be gained, I will go on to visions and revelations from the Lord. I know a man in Christ who fourteen years ago was caught up to the third heaven. Whether it was in the body or out of the body I do not know – God knows. And I know that this man – whether in the body or apart from the body I do not know, but God knows – was caught up to paradise and heard inexpressible things, things that no one is permitted to tell. I will boast about a man like that, but I will not boast about myself, except about my weaknesses. Even if I should choose to boast, I would not be a fool, because I would be speaking the truth. But I refrain, so no one will think more of me than is warranted by what I do or say, or because of these surpassingly great revelations. Therefore, in order to keep me from becoming conceited, I was given a thorn in my flesh, a messenger of Satan, to torment me. Three times I pleaded with the Lord to take it away from me. But he said to me, 'My grace is sufficient for you, for my power is made perfect in weakness.' Therefore I will boast all the more gladly about my weaknesses, so that Christ's power may rest on me. That is why, for Christ's sake, I delight in weaknesses, in insults, in hardships, in persecutions, in difficulties. For when I am weak, then I am strong.

(2 Cor. 12:1–10)

Exploration of vulnerability

This chapter, of all those in this book, was the hardest to write. As I reflected why, I came to the conclusion there were two reasons. The first was the person who is the subject of this last chapter. How could I possibly get into the thoughts and feelings of someone like Paul, that giant of the faith who gave us over a quarter of the New Testament?[1] He was undoubtedly a complex personality, removed from me by a couple of millennia, and he evokes strong responses of varying kinds, from both people of faith and those with none. I didn't want to do him an injustice.

Then there is the topic. The word 'vulnerability' is derived from the Latin word *vulnerare*, which means to wound, and refers to times when we feel ourselves to be at risk in some way, whether physically or emotionally. Ironically, for someone who has spent much of my working life with people who, for varying reasons, were vulnerable, and seeking to help them recognise their strength and courage, it is something I have preferred wherever possible to avoid for myself. That attempt has not always served me well, but I have learned in more recent years to try to offer myself the same compassion I have always wanted to gift others, and to realise that the reasons, from my growing years, that have left me wanting to erect strong defences are, at this point in my life, neither needed nor helpful. That does not mean I enjoy the feeling of exposure and risk that vulnerability entails.

Before I go on to reflect on the topic in general, what was it that brought me to make the link between Paul and vulnerability, which may perhaps be a surprising one, and to explore what might have been some of the causes for it in his life?

Paul was converted, probably around AD34, in the event which gives us the phrase 'Damascus Road experience'.[2] Prior to that he had been, in his own words, 'circumcised on the eighth day, of the people of Israel, of the tribe of Benjamin, a Hebrew of Hebrews; in regard to the law, a Pharisee; as for zeal, persecuting the church; as for righteousness based on the law, faultless.'[3] He had studied under Gamaliel, an esteemed rabbi. As the gospel spread, he saw it as imperative to crush this new movement in order to protect the purity of the Jewish faith, which led to him being present at the death of Stephen, whose story we looked at in the previous chapter. We cannot tell what impact witnessing the manner of Stephen's death and his last

words had, but on that Damascus Road he clearly had an encounter with Jesus which resulted in a radical transformation
and saw him turn that same passion into service for the gospel.
After a time,[4] perhaps spent absorbing the implications of his
new life, he embarked on his new mission, the proclamation of
the good news, using the church in Antioch (in modern-day
Turkey) as a base, and accompanied by Barnabas. Barnabas had
been instrumental in bringing Paul from Tarsus,[5] and although
obviously an impressive figure in his own right,[6] he seemed to
be content to support Paul's ministry and was clearly a huge
encouragement to him. When they argued, because of a disagreement over John Mark,[7] and went their separate ways, it
must have been devastating for Paul. He continued on, with
Silas and then Timothy as companions, but must have missed
Barnabas and his wise counsel.

It is not surprising that Paul was drawn to Corinth on his
second missionary journey. By this time, he was exercising what
we would now call bi-vocational ministry, combining preaching
the gospel with tent-making to support himself. Corinth was a
hugely important city, placed strategically for commercialism,
but was also a byword for drunkenness and dominated by temple worship and prostitution. We know from Acts 18:11 that
Paul stayed in Corinth for at least eighteen months: as verse 18
says that he stayed on 'for some time', it may have been even
longer. The length of his visit there was only exceeded by the
time in Ephesus. Yet that time is summed up by just seventeen
verses, in Acts 18:1–17, so we know relatively little about it.
The church at Corinth was to prove troublesome, with Paul
hearing later of various difficulties and writing several letters,
of which we have just two, and making a visit.[8] This visit was
not a success. Paul's gifting seems to have been primarily evan-
gelistic, and churches fared best when he founded them, but

then left them under the ongoing skilled leadership of others. But that does not mean he did not care deeply about their well-being and progress in the faith, using an image of fatherhood to describe his relationship with them.[9] The failure of the visit distressed Paul deeply.[10]

In addition to these difficulties in relationship, both with Barnabas and the church at Corinth, Paul endured constant criticism, partly because his style of preaching was so different from the grandiose method of itinerant preachers which the ancient world expected, and he had constantly to justify his own credentials.[11] In Ephesus, the conflict over the gospel became violent and Paul had to be prevented from speaking to the rioters.[12] It appears, although they are not recorded in Acts, that the time in Ephesus may also have included a time of imprisonment, perhaps even several.[13] Paul's ministry was, of course, one of constant difficulty as he himself describes:

[I] have worked much harder, been in prison more frequently, been flogged more severely, and been exposed to death again and again. Five times I received from the Jews the forty lashes minus one. Three times I was beaten with rods, once I was pelted with stones, three times I was shipwrecked, I spent a night and a day in the open sea, I have been constantly on the move. I have been in danger from rivers, in danger from bandits, in danger from my fellow Jews, in danger from Gentiles; in danger in the city, in danger in the country, in danger at sea; and in danger from false believers. I have laboured and toiled and have often gone without sleep; I have known hunger and thirst and have often gone without food; I have been cold and naked. Besides everything else, I face daily the pressure of my concern for all the churches.

(2 Cor. 11:23–28)

In addition to all these traumas, it seems that Paul had a significant physical difficulty, which he describes as a 'thorn in [the] flesh'.[14] We might think of a thorn like a splinter, a minor irritation. The word he used, however, *skolops*, more often meant stake, the kind on which criminals were impaled. This implies a severe, savage pain, probably some form of extreme physical suffering rather than either the persecutions or some kind of spiritual temptation, as some have suggested. There have been many theories as to what this might have been: the most popular being epilepsy (seen as demonic in the ancient world), severe and recurring headaches, eye trouble, or repeated bouts of malaria. We simply do not know the answer. What we do know is that Paul repeatedly prayed for it to be removed, but it was not. This man of such great faith faced the mystery and difficulty of unanswered prayer: or more correctly, had to contend with the answer 'no'. However, the response that he believed God gave him was one of hope and reassurance: 'My grace is sufficient for you, for my power is made perfect in weakness.'[15] We will come back to that later.

All of this has taken its toll. In 2 Corinthians 1:8 Paul writes, 'We do not want you to be uninformed, brothers and sisters, about the troubles we experienced in the province of Asia. We were under great pressure, far beyond our ability to endure, so that we despaired of life itself.' The latter phrase is one related to appealing a death sentence. In the course of 2 Corinthians, Paul uses images of a procession of captives,[16] a gospel veiled to the perishing,[17] a clay jar[18] and a tent which is wearing out.[19] The whole letter is shot through with Paul's extreme vulnerability.

It is arguable that in some generations and cultures, vulnerability has been seen as something to be avoided, or at least kept hidden. I suspect this may have been the case for Paul, before the events in Asia forced him to recognise it. One of the reasons for this tendency is that we believe in several myths about vulnerability. The first is that we can somehow avoid it. That is ultimately not possible. Health issues, ageing, emotional challenges, or difficulty in relationships happen to us all at some point in our lives, whatever defences we might try to place around ourselves. These life events leave us vulnerable cognitively, emotionally, socially, physically, or a combination of them. If we try to avoid it or disguise it, the armour we wear can be a hindrance: as someone once said to me, a suit of armour is essential in warfare but a hindrance when it comes to making love. Life brings with it vulnerability, from before birth and until its end. We cannot escape it.

Another myth is that vulnerability is the same as weakness. We are hopefully able to recognise the courage it takes for others to be vulnerable and treat them with care when they open up to us, seeing it as a privilege. Yet we can see it as a failing in ourselves when we need to share a difficulty. So we shield ourselves, perhaps suppressing our discomfort with alcohol, TV, or food. There may be cultural variations here: the idea of suppressing emotions was important, for example, to both the Spartans and Stoics. We speak about a 'stiff upper lip', a refusal to cry or display emotions as being a British trait, though this has not always been the case.[20] Other cultures disguise their emotions less.

A final myth I want to mention is the erroneous belief that to be vulnerable with others means that we have to tell everyone everything. However, that is not what vulnerability is. To be open and honest with another person, there need to be boundaries to make it a safe place. These may be of confidentiality, such as in a helping relationship, and of trust, such as with a friend. There may be boundaries too, in the amount and nature of what we share. Even with those we trust, we do not need to say everything. The birth of my first child was a very difficult and traumatic one, and in time a friend offered to let me tell the story. He happened to be male, and so while I was able to be very vulnerable emotionally, and his listening was very healing, there were aspects of the experience I chose not to talk about.

I have been profoundly impacted in my own journey with vulnerability by the work of Brené Brown. She is a researcher who has spent more than twenty years studying vulnerability, courage and shame, working with many groups both in research and teaching. She has freely admitted, not least in her 2010 Ted Talk,[21] which went viral, that she hates vulnerability and had hoped to find a way to eliminate it through her research. What in fact she discovered is that vulnerability is necessary for true human connection, involving as it does uncertainty, risk and emotional exposure. She talks with both humour and empathy about how essential but how difficult vulnerability is, requiring us to be very courageous.

Part of Brené Brown's research has concentrated on our ability to feel that we are enough: one of the things that prevents us from being vulnerable is our fear of the shame we will experience if we are 'outed' as not good enough, not clever enough and so on. This touches perhaps on a difference of perspective theologically. There is a vast difference between a view of our fallen nature that is described as 'total depravity', which sees us as having nothing good about us and, in contrast, one that sees us as fallen, yes, but still beloved children – what a friend once described as still a designer item despite having a flaw. I know for myself that coming to terms with, even embracing, my vulnerability, has gone hand in hand with an ongoing journey to discover what it really means to be, first and foremost, a loved and accepted child of God.

For Paul, the result of his struggle with vulnerability led to the most profound realisation: that God's 'power is made perfect in weakness' in a way that it cannot be in our supposed 'strength'.

This is not always the prevailing message in the modern church, where 'success' is more often seen as reflected in the size of the congregation or buildings. At a personal level too, how often in our churches is the question 'How are you?' greeted with 'I'm fine', almost as a reflex response? Paul's discovery suggests that to fail to both recognise and work with our vulnerability, individually and corporately, means we may be missing an opportunity for God to work in the very things we are trying to suppress. While we will all differ in how much, and with whom, we are willing to be vulnerable (and we can risk either of the extremes I mentioned in the chapter on honesty, of inappropriate openness in every setting or rigid unassailable defences), there need to be places somewhere where we can be honest and vulnerable. It is a tragedy if we or others feel church is the last place we can be that. Our churches need to be places of safety where we do not have to have it all together and can admit that we are struggling without fear either of judgement or of others rushing in with a Bible verse 'prescription' rather than walking alongside us.[22] It may be then that we too, like Paul, can discover that when our own strength runs out, in our vulnerability we can be surprised by the depths of God's grace, and find his power displayed in a new way which we had never expected.

Reflection questions

- What thoughts and feelings does the word 'vulnerable' evoke in you?
- What might God's grace being enough for you look like in your current situation?
- Who are those in your life who you can be vulnerable with, and who gifts you their vulnerability?

Final Thoughts

So we have reached the end of our journey, taking a glimpse at the lives of some of the biblical 'heroes and villains' and, I hope, recognising that the qualities we see in them are there within us too. Some of those qualities are lurking mainly unseen in us, but need to be brought into the light and owned so that God can, like a skilled surgeon, deal with them as his work of transformation in us continues. Some of them he wants to grow in us even more, gifts of his remarkable grace!

As I said in the Introduction, the biblical characters are as complex as we are, and I love the honesty of the Bible in showing that in all its glorious and sometimes shocking reality. If it did not do so, it would not draw us in as it does. In its pages we see ourselves mirrored: the heroic moments of sacrifice and the devastating moments of failure, the times of running away from God and the times of catching his heart and allowing it to enlarge our own.

I hope that this book has helped you to grow a little in your understanding of the Bible characters we have explored together. My prayer is also that this book may have helped you above all to see yourself as you are, a loved child of the God of grace who takes the sometimes unpromising material of flawed human lives to use for his glory.

I would love to hear your story, and any comments you might like to make about the book. If you are on Facebook, search for the page Finding Our Voice, Held in Your Bottle, Heroes or Villains, or I can be contacted on heroesorvillainsbook@gmail.com.

May you continue to journey into becoming all of who God has made you to be.

God bless you.

Acknowledgements

There are so many people without whom this book would never have made it to publication, some I can acknowledge here and so many others whose names may not appear but who have had a significant part to play in my life.

I owe so much to the team at Authentic, who took a risk with my first book, *Finding Our Voice*, and continue to be a wonderful support in my writing. I could never have done any of it without them and they are fantastic to work with. Sheila Jacobs, who has now edited all three of my books, is a joy to work with.

My huge thanks go to Geoff Colmer for being willing to write the Foreword and for all the ways he has ministered both to me and to others.

Thank you to all those people who were willing to endorse the book – I really appreciated it.

A special shout out to my friend of more than fifty years, Rachel Johnson, who checked every chapter and encouraged me along the way. I think I have finally learned to put the footnote number after the punctuation!

David Mayne is always a fantastic support with his many chats via Messenger. His friendship is such a gift.

Liz Connelly, Laura Gilmore and Ali Tin gave helpful suggestions in the early days and the UK Women in Baptist ministry Facebook group are a great support.

My family as always are the underpinning: Malc who is tirelessly supportive in so many ways, and Amy and Vali, Faith and Gabriel, Helen and Ross who all bring me so much joy. My prayer is always that each of you draw closer to Jesus.

And always, of course, to you, Jesus, all the glory goes. If any of the lovely qualities that I have written about in this book are there at all in me, it is because of you, and thank you so much that you forgive the rest. Your grace to me is beyond words.

Bibliography and Further Reading

Adorno, T.W., Else Frenkel-Brunswik, Daniel J. Levinson, and R. Nevitt Sanford. *The Authoritarian Personality* (London: Verso, 2019).

Allport, Gordon W., *The Nature of Prejudice: 25th Anniversary Edition* (New York: Basic Books, 1979).

Allport, Gordon W., *Personality and Social Encounter* (Boston, MA: Beacon Press, 1960).

Ariely, Dan, *The Honest Truth About Dishonesty: How We Lie to Everyone – Especially Ourselves* (London: HarperCollins, 2013).

Arnott, John and Carol, *Grace and Forgiveness* (Toronto: Catch the Fire, 2015).

Atkinson, David J., and David H. Field. *New Dictionary of Christian Ethics and Pastoral Theology* (Leicester: Inter-Varsity Press, 1995).

Bailey, Kenneth E., *Jesus Through Middle Eastern Eyes* (London: SPCK, 2008).

Barclay, William, *The Gospel of John Vol. 1* (Edinburgh: The Saint Andrew Press, 1955).

Barclay, William, *The Gospel of John Vol. 2* (Edinburgh: The Saint Andrew Press, 1955).

Barclay, William, *The Gospel of Luke* (Edinburgh: The Saint Andrew Press, 1953).

Barclay, William, *The Gospel of Matthew Vol. 1* (Edinburgh: The Saint Andrew Press, 1956).

Barclay, William, *The Gospel of Matthew Vol. 2* (Edinburgh: The Saint Andrew Press, 1957).

Barclay, William, *The Letters to the Corinthians* (Edinburgh: The Saint Andrew Press, 1975).

Barr, Beth Allison, *Making of Biblical Womanhood: How the Subjugation of Women Became Gospel Truth* (Ada, MI: Brazos Press, 2021).

Benner, David G., *Surrender to Love: Discovering the Heart of Christian Spirituality* (Expanded) (The Spiritual Journey) (Leicester: Inter-Varsity Press, 2015).

Bowlby, John, *Attachment* (London: Random House, 1997).

Bowlby, John, *A Secure Base* (Abingdon: Routledge, 2005).

Brown, Brené, *Dare to Lead* (London: Penguin Random House, 2018).

Brown, Brené, *Daring Greatly: How the Courage to Be Vulnerable Transforms the Way We Live, Love, Parent, and Lead* (London: Penguin, 2013).

Brown, Brené, *Rising Strong* (London: Penguin Random House, 2015).

Brown, Brené, *The Gifts of Imperfection* (Center City, MN: Hazelden, 2020).

Chan, Francis, *Crazy Love: Overwhelmed by a Relentless God* (Colorado Springs, CO: David C. Cook, 2013).

Clance, Pauline Rose, *The Imposter Phenomenon: Overcoming the Fear That Haunts Your Success* (Atlanta, GA: Peachtree Publications, 1985).

Dixon, Thomas, *Weeping Britannia: Portrait of a Nation in Tears* (Oxford: Oxford University Press, 2016).

Dormandy, Richard, *Shabby Treasure: St Paul's Emergence Through Personal and Ministerial Crisis* (Pimlico: Brindley Books, 2006).

Dormandy, Richard, *The Madness of St Paul: How St Paul Discovered the Love of God* (Chawton: Redemptorist Publications, 2011).

Ellison, H.L., 'Jonah' in Frank E. Gaebelein, *The Expositor's Bible Commentary Volume Seven* (Grand Rapids, MI: Zondervan, 1985).

Foster, Richard, *Money, Sex and Power* (London: Hodder & Stoughton, 2009).

Frankl, Viktor E., *Man's Search for Meaning* (London: Rider, 2004).

Freyd, Jennifer, *Betrayal Trauma: Logic of Forgetting Childhood Abuse: The Logic of Forgetting Childhood Abuse* (Cambridge, MA: Harvard University Press, 1998).

Galinsky, Adam, and Maurice Schweitzer. *Friend & Foe: When to Cooperate, When to Compete, and How to Succeed at Both* (New York: Random House Business, 2016).

Goldingay, John, *1 & 2 Kings for Everyone* (London: SPCK, 2011).

Goldingay, John, *1 & 2 Chronicles for Everyone* (London: SPCK, 2012).

Goldingay, John, *After Eating the Apricot* (Carlisle: Paternoster, 1996).

Goldingay, John, *Genesis for Everyone* (London: SPCK, 2010).

Goldingay, John, *Joshua, Judges, and Ruth for Everyone* (London: SPCK, 2011).

Goldingay, John, *Men Behaving Badly* (Carlisle: Paternoster, 2000).

Goldingay, John, *Walk On: Life, Loss, Trust, and Other Realities* (Ada, MI: Baker Academic, 2002).

Grant, J., and J. Crawley. *Transference and Projection: Mirrors to the Self* (Buckingham: Open University Press, 2002).

Green, Michael, *The Message of Matthew* (Leicester: Inter-Varsity Press, 1988).

Hamilton, Adam, *Unafraid: Living with Courage and Hope in Uncertain Times* (Colorado Springs, CO: Convergent Books, 2018).

Hamley, Isabelle, *Embracing Justice* (London: SPCK, 2021).

Harvey, A.E., *Renewal Through Suffering: A Study of 2 Corinthians* (Edinburgh: T&T Clark, 1996).

Hofmann, W., and L.F. Nordgren, eds. *The Psychology of Desire* (New York: The Guilford Press, 2015).

Jacobs, Michael, *The Presenting Past: The Core of Psychodynamic Counselling and Therapy* (Maidenhead: Open University Press, 2012).

Kendall, Jeannie, *Finding our Voice* (Milton Keynes: Authentic Media, 2019).

Kendall, Jeannie, *Held in Your Bottle* (Milton Keynes: Authentic Media, 2021).

Kendall, R.T., *Total Forgiveness: Achieving God's Greatest Challenge* (London: Hodder & Stoughton, 2010).

Luskin, Frederic, *Forgive for Good: A Proven Prescription for Health and Happiness* (New York: HarperCollins, 2003).

Martin, Jessica, *Holiness and Desire: What Makes Us Who We Are?* (Norwich: Canterbury Press, 2020).

Maslow, Abraham H., *A Theory of Human Motivation* (Eastford, CT: Martino Fine Books, 2013).

Maslow, Abraham H., *Toward a Psychology of Being* (Floyd, VA: Sublime Books, 2014).

Miller, Christian B., *Honesty: The Philosophy and Psychology of a Neglected Virtue* (New York: Oxford University Press, 2021).

Milne, Bruce, *The Message of John* (Leicester: Inter-Varsity Press, 1993).

Musters, Claire, and Steve Musters. *Grace-Filled Marriage: Strengthened and Transformed Through God's Redemptive Love* (Milton Keynes: Authentic Media, 2021).

Nouwen, Henri, *Bread for the Journey* (San Francisco, CA: HarperOne, 2009 Kindle version).

Nouwen, Henri, *The Return of the Prodigal Son* (London: Darton, Longman & Todd, 1994).

Nye, Joseph S., *Soft Power: The Means to Success in World Politics* (New York: PublicAffairs, 2004).

Ortego, Alicia, *Honesty is My Superpower: A Kid's Book About Telling the Truth and Overcoming Lying* (Independently published, 2022).

Paharia, Rajat, *Loyalty 3.0: How to Revolutionize Customer and Employee Engagement with Big Data and Gamification* (New York: McGraw-Hill, 2013).

Patterson, Richard D., and Hermann J. Austel, '1 and 2 Kings' in Frank E. Gaebelein, *The Expositor's Bible Commentary Volume Four* (Grand Rapids, MI: Zondervan, 1988).

Payne, J. Barton, '1 and 2 Chronicles' in Frank E. Gaebelein, *The Expositor's Bible Commentary Volume Four* (Grand Rapids, MI: Zondervan, 1988).

Payne, Tony, and Geoff Robson. *The Generosity Project* (Youngstown, OH: Matthias Media, 2020).

Percey, Andy, *Made to Belong: Moving Beyond Tribalism to Find Our True Connection in God* (Milton Keynes: Authentic Media, 2021).

Peterson, Christopher, and Martin E.P. Seligman. *Character Strengths and Virtues: A Handbook and Classification Vol. 1* (New York: Oxford University Press, 2004).

Peterson, Eugene H., *The Message of David* (London: Marshall Pickering, 1997).

Plass, Adrian, *Blind Spots in the Bible* (Oxford: Bible Reading Fellowship, 2006).

Pope Francis, *The Name of God is Mercy* (Basingstoke: Bluebird, 2016).

Rice, Ruth, *Slow Down, Show Up and Pray: Simple Shared Habits to Renew Wellbeing in Our Local Communities* (Milton Keynes: Authentic Media, 2021).

Rice, Ruth, *The A-Z of Wellbeing: Finding Your Personal Toolkit for Peace and Wholeness* (Milton Keynes: Authentic Media, 2022).

Ryan, M.J., *Radical Generosity: Unlock the Transformative Power of Giving* (Newburyport, MA: Conari Press, 2018).

Sailhamer, John, 'Genesis' in Frank E. Gaebelein, *The Expositor's Bible Commentary Volume Two* (Grand Rapids, MI: Zondervan, 1990).

Shapiro, Shauna L., *Rewire Your Mind: Discover the Science and Practice of Mindfulness* (London: Aster, 2020).

Smedes, Lewis B., *The Art of Forgiving: When You Need to Forgive and Don't Know How* (New York: Ballantine Books, 1996).

Smedes, Lewis B., *Forgive and Forget: Healing the Hurts We Don't Deserve* (New York: HarperCollins, 1996).

Stibbe, Mark, *From Orphans to Heirs: Celebrating Our Spiritual Adoption* (Abingdon: Bible Reading Fellowship, 2005).

Stott, John, *The Message of Acts* (Leicester: Inter-Varsity Press, 1990).

Tenney, Merrill C., *The Expositor's Bible Commentary John* (Grand Rapids, MI: Zondervan, 1995).

Trible, Phyllis, and Letty M. Russell, eds. *Hagar, Sarah, and Their Children: Jewish, Christian, and Muslim Perspectives* (Louisville, KY: Westminster/John Knox Press, 2006).

Trible, Phyllis, *Texts of Terror (40th Anniversary Edition): Literary-Feminist Readings of Biblical Narratives* (Minneapolis, MN: Fortress Press, 2022).

Tutu, Desmond M., *No Future Without Forgiveness* (London: Rider, 1999).

Watson, David, *Discipleship* (London: Hodder & Stoughton, 2014).

Wilcock, Michael, *The Message of Luke* (Leicester: Inter-Varsity Press, 1979).

Wolf, Herbert, 'Judges' in Frank E. Gaebelein, *The Expositor's Bible Commentary Volume Two* (Grand Rapids, MI: Zondervan, 1990).

Worthington, Everett L., *Five Steps to Forgiveness: The Art and Science of Forgiving* (New York: Crown, 2001).

Worthington, Everett L., *Forgiveness and Reconciliation: Theory and Application* (New York: Routledge, 2006).

Worthington, Everett L., *Forgiving and Reconciling: Finding Our Way Through Cultural Challenges* (Revised) (Leicester: Inter-Varsity Press, 2003).

Wright, N.T., *Matthew for Everyone: Part 1, Chapters 1–15* (London: SPCK, 2004).

Wright, N.T., *Matthew for Everyone: Part 2, Chapters 16–28* (London: SPCK, 2002).

Wright, N.T., *John for Everyone: Part 1, Chapters 1–10* (London: SPCK, 2004).

Wright, N.T., *John for Everyone: Part 2, Chapters 11–21* (London: SPCK, 2002).

Wright, N.T., *Paul for Everyone: 2 Corinthians* (London: SPCK, 2004).

Youngblood, Ronald F., '1 and 2 Samuel' in Frank E. Gaebelein, *The Expositor's Bible Commentary Volume Three* (Grand Rapids, MI: Zondervan, 1992).

Websites

General

https://bible.org/ (accessed 18 May 2022)

https://www.nhs.uk/mental-health/self-help/tips-and-support/mindfulness/ (accessed 8 April 2022)

https://psychoanalysis.org.uk/our-authors-and-theorists/melanie-klein (accessed 12 December 2022)

Dissatisfaction

http://www.lifeandpsychology.com/2010/06/self-satisfaction-ultimate-goal-of-life.html (accessed 8 April 2022)

https://positivepsychology.com/life-satisfaction/ (accessed 8 April 2022)

https://www.simplypsychology.org/maslow.html (accessed 10 April 2022)

Resentment

https://www.goodtherapy.org/blog/psychpedia/resentment
(accessed 19 April 2022)

Desire

http://justus.anglican.org/~ss/commonworship/word/morn-
ingbcp.html (accessed 1 May 2022)

http://www.commonprayer.org/offices/absol.cfm (accessed 2
May 2022)

https://plato.stanford.edu/entries/desire/ (accessed 2 May 2022)

Loyalty

https://www.destinationcrm.com/Articles/Web-Exclusives/
Viewpoints/The-Psychology-of-Loyalty-100641.aspx
(accessed 6 May 2022)

https://www.psychologytoday.com/gb/blog/the-main-ingredient/
201901/who-deserves-your-loyalty (accessed 6 May 2022)

https://www.thoughtco.com/adult-attachment-styles-
4774974 (accessed 6 May 2022)

Greed

https://www.nhs.uk/live-well/addiction-support/addiction-
what-is-it/ (accessed 10 May 2022)

https://recovered.org/addiction/addiction-and-genetics (accessed 10 May 2022)

https://www.christianity.com/wiki/sin/what-are-the-seven-deadly-sins.html (accessed 10 May 2022)

Mercy

https://www.biblesociety.org.uk/explore-the-bible/bible-articles/what-does-the-bible-say-about-the-mercy-of-jesus/ (accessed 20 May 2022)

https://www.desiringgod.org/articles/have-mercy-on-me (accessed 20 May 2022)

https://www.youtube.com/watch?v=H_8y0WLm78U (Ted Talk The Price of Shame) (accessed 20 May 2022)

https://www.crosswalk.com/devotionals/daily-hope-with-rick-warren/seven-characteristics-of-mercy-daily-hope-with-rick-warren-february-3-2019.html (accessed 20 May 2022)

Protest

https://associationforjewishstudies.org/publications-research/ajs-perspectives/the-protest-issue/prophetic-protest-in-the-hebrew-bible (accessed 25 April 2022)

https://www.eauk.org/idea/should-christians-protest.cfm (accessed 25 April 2022)

https://calvarychapel.com/posts/five-ways-to-protest-like-a-christian (accessed 25 April 2022) https://www.insider.com/why-people-protest-according-to-science-2020-6 (accessed 25 April 2022)

https://www.beliefnet.com/faiths/christianity/should-christians-protest.aspx (accessed 29 April 2022)

http://www.worldevangelicals.org/pdf/Violence_Abortion_Clinics_Schirrmacher_English_112009.pdf (accessed 29 April 2022)

Wisdom

https://www.bibleodyssey.org/passages/related-articles/what-is-wisdom-literature (accessed 20 June 2022)

http://www.wisdompage.com/AnOverviewOfThePsychologyOfWisdom.html (accessed 20 June 2022)

https://www.youtube.com/watch?v=obqedyeUcwk (accessed 20 June 2022)

https://positivepsychology.com/wisdom/ (accessed 20 June 2022)

https://evidencebasedwisdom.com/2015/09/20/the-berlin-wisdom-paradigm-an-expert-knowledge-system/ (accessed 20 June 2022)

Power

https://softpower30.com/what-is-soft-power/ (accessed 20 June 2022)

https://www.biblicalarchaeology.org/daily/people-cultures-in-the-bible/people-in-the-bible/how-bad-was-jezebel/ (accessed 23 June 2022) https://www.mindtools.com/pages/article/newLDR_56.htm (accessed 24 June 2022)

https://www.wired.com/2010/08/the-psychology-of-power/ (accessed 24 June 2022)

https://www.bbc.com/news/health-19842100 (accessed 24 June 2022)

https://about-history.com/the-role-of-the-jester-in-the-medieval-society-how-he-can-make-you-laugh-or-even-die/ (accessed 24 June 2022)

https://academyofideas.com/2020/07/the-psychology-of-power-how-to-dethrone-tyrants/ (accessed 24 June 2022)

https://www.biblestudytools.com/dictionaries/bakers-evangelical-dictionary/power.html (accessed 24 June 2022)

Prejudice

https://www.newworldencyclopedia.org/entry/Prejudice (accessed 23 May 2022)

https://www.simplypsychology.org/prejudice.html (accessed 23 May 2022)

https://secure.understandingprejudice.org/apa/english/ (accessed 23 May 2022)

https://www.myjewishlearning.com/article/jonah-yom-kippur/ (accessed 26 May 2022)

https://jewishstandard.timesofisrael.com/the-book-of-jonah-and-yom-kippur/ (accessed 26 May 2022)

https://www.ministrymagazine.org/archive/1988/09/the-christian-and-prejudice (accessed 1 June 2022)

Courage

https://www.psychologytoday.com/us/blog/the-mindful-self-express/201208/the-six-attributes-courage (accessed 8 June 2022)

https://www.bbc.co.uk/programmes/m000x4wf (All in the Mind) (accessed 8 June 2022)

https://www.psychologytoday.com/us/blog/cultivating-courage/201011/the-meaning-courage (accessed 8 June 2022)

https://www.mequilibrium.com/resources/the-psychology-of-courage/ (accessed 8 June 2022)

Patience

https://www.psychologytoday.com/us/blog/emotional-freedom/201209/the-power-patience (accessed 4 July 2022)

https://www.compellingtruth.org/Bible-patience.html (accessed 6 July 2022)

https://www.christianitytoday.com/biblestudies/articles/spiritual formation/virtue-of-patience.html (accessed 6 July 2022)

Witness

https://www.cru.org/us/en/train-and-grow/10-basic-steps/7-the-christian-and-witnessing.html (accessed 7 June 2022)

Generosity

https://www.psychologytoday.com/us/blog/master-your-success/202001/the-real-challenge-generosity (accessed 13 June 2022)

https://www.psychalive.org/benefits-of-generosity/ https://www.psychalive.org/benefits-of-generosity/ (accessed 13 June 2022)

https://exploringyourmind.com/generosity-from-a-psychological-perspective/ (accessed 14 June 2022)

https://www.medicalnewstoday.com/articles/322940 (accessed 14 June 2022)

https://time.com/4857777/generosity-happiness-brain/ (accessed 15 June 2022)

https://blogs.scientificamerican.com/literally-psyched/the-psychology-behind-gift-giving-and-generosity/ (accessed 15 June 2022)

https://www.theguardian.com/science/2015/jan/26/rationing-ravens-merciful-monkeys-can-animals-be-altruistic (accessed 14 June 2022)

https://www.nature.com/articles/ncomms15964.pdf (accessed 15 June 2022)

https://ggsc.berkeley.edu/images/uploads/GGSC-JTF_White_Paper-Generosity-FINAL.pdf (accessed 15 June 2022)

Betrayal

https://www.jewishencyclopedia.com/articles/9034-judas-maccabeus (accessed 19 July 2022)

https://synapse.ucsf.edu/articles/2017/12/05/psychology-betrayal (accessed 19 July 2022)

https://psychology.iresearchnet.com/social-psychology/interpersonal-relationships/betrayal/ (accessed 19 July 2022 and 30 July 2022)

https://www.psychologytoday.com/us/blog/anger-in-the-age-entitlement/201401/trust-and-betrayal (accessed 19 July 2022)

Insecurity

https://www.biblicalarchaeology.org/daily/people-cultures-in-the-bible/people-in-the-bible/herod-antipas-in-the-bible-and-beyond/ (accessed 28 August 2022)

https://jewishencyclopedia.com/ (accessed 28 June 2022)

https://www.choosingtherapy.com/insecurity/ (accessed 29 June 2022)

https://www.berkeleywellbeing.com/insecurity.html (accessed 29 June 2022)

https://www.berkeleywellbeing.com/imposter-syndrome.html (accessed 29 June 2022)

https://www.gotquestions.org/Bible-insecurity.html (accessed 29 June 2022)

https://www.psychologytoday.com/us/basics/perfectionism (accessed 2 July 2022)

https://aleteia.org/2017/09/12/how-the-roman-practice-of-adoption-sheds-light-on-what-st-paul-was-talking-about/ (accessed 2 July 2022)

Surrender

https://www.britannica.com/biography/Pontius-Pilate (accessed 9 July 2022)

https://www.history.com/news/why-pontius-pilate-executed-jesus (accessed 9 July 2022)

http://news.bbc.co.uk/1/hi/uk/1273594.stm (accessed 9 July 2022)

https://www.psychologytoday.com/us/blog/finding-your-voice/201307/the-art-surrender (accessed 9 July 2022)

https://www.learnreligions.com/jewish-hand-washing-rituals-2076317 (accessed 13 July 2022)

Honesty

https://www.ivritalk.com/hebrew-days-of-the-week/ (accessed 22 July 22)

http://emotionalprocessing.org/somatization/ (accessed 25 July 2022)

https://www.goodtherapy.org/blog/psychpedia/honesty (accessed 25 July 2022)

https://www.psychologytoday.com/us/blog/the-nature-deception/202012/the-evolution-honesty (accessed 25 July 2022)

https://www.theguardian.com/science/2006/jun/28/psychology.uknews (accessed 25 July 2022)

https://psyche.co/ideas/more-than-just-truth-telling-honesty-is-a-virtue-to-cultivate (accessed 26 July 2022)

Forgiveness

https://hebrewwordlessons.com/ (accessed 30 July 2022)

https://positivepsychology.com/psychology-of-forgiveness/ (accessed 30 July 2022)

https://www.psychologytoday.com/us/blog/the-addiction-connection/201409/the-psychology-forgiveness (accessed 30 July 2022)

https://www.theforgivenessproject.com/ (accessed 30 July 2022)

https://positivepsychology.com/forgiveness-benefits/ (accessed 30 July 2022)

Vulnerability

https://www.youtube.com/watch?v=iCvmsMzlF7o&t=37s (Brené Brown Ted Talk The Power of Vulnerability) (accessed 2 August 2022)

https://www.renewwellbeing.org.uk/ (accessed 6 August 2022)

https://crm.org/articles/brene-brown-vulnerability (accessed 6 August 2022)

https://brenebrown.com/podcasts/?refinementList%5Btopics%5D%5B0%5D=Vulnerability&pagination=1 (accessed 6 August 2022)

Notes

Introduction

[1] If you are unfamiliar with them, they are a team of fictional super heroes based on the Marvel comic books.

[2] First published in three parts in 1954 and 1955 by Allen & Unwin. The films were released in 2001 (*The Fellowship of the Ring*), 2002 (*The Two Towers*) and 2003 (*The Return of the King*). They were produced and distributed by New Line Cinema with the co-production of WingNut Films.

[3] Rom. 7:19.

[4] For an introduction to her work, see Hannah Segal, *Introduction to the Work of Melanie Klein* (Karnac Classics) (Abingdon: Routledge, 2018).

[5] 1 Sam. 13:14.

Chapter 1: Adam and Eve

[1] See for example https://financesonline.com/10-lottery-winners-stories-dont-make-the-same-mistakes-they-did/ (accessed 8 April 2022).

[2] Gen. 2:15.

[3] John Sailhamer, 'Genesis' in Frank E. Gaebelein, *The Expositor's Bible Commentary Volume Two* (Grand Rapids, MI: Zondervan, 1990), p. 45.

4   Abraham Maslow, *Toward a Psychology of Being* (Floyd, VA: Sublime Books, 2014), pp. 5–6.

5   See https://positivepsychology.com/life-satisfaction/ (accessed 8 April 2022).

6   Viktor E. Frankl, *Man's Search for Meaning* (London: Rider, 2004).

7   Gen. 3:12.

8   Phil. 4:11.

9   Phil. 4:13.

Chapter 2: Cain

1   Passive-aggressive behaviour is where we appear amiable but our behaviour, often subconsciously, is stubborn, procrastinating, or sabotaging: a 'smiling assassin'.

2   Matt. 5:23–24.

3   See Jeannie Kendall, *Finding Our Voice* (Milton Keynes: Authentic Media, 2019), pp. 50–62 and Chapter 19 of this book.

Chapter 3: Samson

1   The others are gluttony, greed, sloth, wrath, envy and pride.

2   See chapters on Adam and Eve, and Cain and Abel.

3   Interestingly, research shows 37 per cent of people mistake thirst for hunger, eating when they need to drink. See https://pkdcure.org/hunger-vs-thirst/ (accessed 5 December 2022).

4   Rom. 7:19.

5   See https://plato.stanford.edu/entries/desire/ (accessed 2 May 2022).

6   Eph. 1:18–20.

7   Henri Nouwen, *Bread for the Journey* (San Francisco, CA: HarperOne, 2009 Kindle version), p. 116.

8   Judg. 16:28,30.

9   Heb. 11:32.

10 Mark 12:31.
11 1 Cor. 6:19–20.
12 Matt. 10:38–39.
13 Ps. 37:4.

Chapter 4: Ruth

1 See John Bowlby, *Attachment* (London: Random House, 1997) and *A Secure Base* (Abingdon: Routledge, 2005).
2 Rajat Paharia, *Loyalty 3.0: How to Revolutionize Customer and Employee Engagement with Big Data and Gamification* (Maidenhead: McGraw-Hill, 2013).
3 Matt. 6:24.
4 Jas 4:4.
5 Rom. 12:5.
6 See Matt. 1:5.

Chapter 5: Eli's Sons

1 1 Sam. 1:14.
2 See https://www.nhs.uk/live-well/addiction-support/addiction-what-is-it/ (accessed 10 May 2022).
3 https://recovered.org/addiction/addiction-and-genetics (accessed 10 May 2022).
4 See https://www.ncbi.nlm.nih.gov/pmc/articles/PMC3124340/ (accessed 10 May 2022).
5 See https://www.nhs.uk/mental-health/conditions/hoarding-disorder/ (accessed 5 December 2022).
6 Luke 12:15.
7 1 Tim. 6:10.
8 Luke 16:14.
9 Gal. 5:22–23.
10 See 1 Cor. 9:25–27; Rom. 7:24–25.

Chapter 6: David

1 1 Sam. 20:15.
2 1 Sam. 24:5.
3 Ps. 51:1.
4 Gen. 3:21.
5 Exod. 33:19; 34:6–7.
6 Luke 18:13; Luke 17:13; Mark 10:47.
7 Luke 5:8.
8 John 21:15–19.
9 John 7:53 – 8:11. See Kendall, *Finding Our Voice*, Chapter 7 for more on this story.
10 https://www.youtube.com/watch?v=H_8y0WLm78U&t=175s (accessed 20 May 2022).
11 Lam. 3:22–23.
12 1 Tim. 1:16; Eph. 2:4–5.
13 Heb. 4:16.
14 Hos. 6:6.
15 Mic. 6:8.
16 Matt. 5:7.
17 Jas 2:13.

Chapter 7: Rizpah

1 See https://www.youtube.com/watch?v=3P_s3ChZlRY (accessed 5 December 2022).
2 There are two people named Mephibosheth in this story. One is the lame son of Jonathan, David's friend. David spares him – see the chapter on mercy. The other Mephibosheth is the son of Rizpah and Saul.
3 See Luke 13:1–5; John 9:1–3.
4 https://www.insider.com/why-people-protest-according-to-science-2020-6 (accessed 25 April 2022).

[5] Luke 8:1–3; Luke 10:39.

[6] Matt. 21:12–13.

[7] See http://www.worldevangelicals.org/pdf/Violence_Abortion_Clinics_Schirrmacher_English_112009.pdf (accessed 29 April 2022).

[8] Rom. 13:1.

[9] See Acts 4, in particular verses 18–20.

[10] Prov. 31:8–9.

Chapter 8: Solomon

[1] See http://www.wisdompage.com/AnOverviewOfThePsychologyOfWisdom.html (accessed 20 June 2022).

[2] Christopher Peterson and Martin E.P. Seligman, *Character Strengths and Virtues: A Handbook and Classification* (Vol 1) (Oxford: Oxford University Press, 2004), p. 39.

[3] Prov. 3:5.

[4] Jas 3:17.

[5] Jas 3:13.

[6] 2 Chr. 1:10.

[7] 1 Kgs 3:9.

[8] 1 Kgs 3:13–14.

[9] Phil. 1:9–10.

[10] See for example Prov. 23.

[11] Prov. 23:1–2.

[12] Prov. 8:1; Prov. 8:27; Prov. 8:15–19.

[13] Luke 2:40; see also Luke 2:52.

[14] See for example Mark 6:2.

[15] Matt. 12:42.

[16] 1 Cor. 1:24.

[17] John 1:2–3.

[18] See 1 Cor. 1:18–21.

[19] Jas 1:5.

Chapter 9: Jezebel

[1] 2 Kgs 9:30–31.

[2] Source https://www.mindtools.com/pages/article/newLDR_56 .htm (accessed 24 June 2022).

[3] See https://about-history.com/the-role-of-the-jester-in-the-medieval-society-how-he-can-make-you-laugh-or-even-die/ (accessed 24 June 2022).

[4] See https://www.wired.com/2010/08/the-psychology-of-power/ (accessed 24 June 2022).

[5] Such as at the Royal Society of Medicine conference, entitled 'The Intoxication of Power' on Tuesday, 9 October 2012. Reported in https://www.bbc.com/news/health-19842100 (accessed 24 June 2022).

[6] See J. Grant and J. Crawley, *Transference and Projection: Mirrors to the Self* (Buckingham: Open University Press, 2002) and Michael Jacobs, *The Presenting Past: The Core of Psychodynamic Counselling and Therapy* (Maidenhead: Open University Press, 2012).

[7] Rom. 1:20.

[8] Jer. 27:5.

[9] Job 38:1.

[10] Isa. 40:29.

[11] Luke 1:35.

[12] See for example Mark 4:35–41; Mark 8:22–26; Mark 5:1–20.

[13] Eph. 1:19–20.

[14] Rom. 1:16.

[15] Gal. 5:22–23.

[16] 1 Cor. 2:4.

[17] 2 Cor. 12:9.

Chapter 10: Jonah

[1] Gen. 12:2–3.

[2] Jonah 1:9.

[3] Jonah 4:2.

4 Jonah 4:11.

5 See Grant and Crawley, *Transference and Projection: Mirrors to the Self.*

6 T.W. Adorno, Else Frenkel-Brunswik, Daniel J. Levinson, R. Nevitt Sanford, *The Authoritarian Personality* (London: Verso, 2019). See also Gordon W. Allport, *The Nature Of Prejudice: 25th Anniversary Edition* (New York: Basic Books, 1979).

7 For further details of the study, see https://www.simplypsychology.org/robbers-cave.html (accessed 5 December 2022).

8 Gordon W. Allport, *Personality and Social Encounter* (Boston, MA: Beacon Press, 1960), p. 257.

9 Luke 15:11–32.

10 Mark 2:13–17; Luke 8:1–3; Luke 10:38–42.

11 Luke 7:1–10.

12 John 4:1–42.

13 Acts 10:34.

14 Gal. 3:28.

Chapter 11: Mary

1 A literal translation of Luke 1:28.

2 https://www.bbc.co.uk/programmes/m000x4wf (accessed 8 June 2022).

Chapter 12: Simeon

1 Heb. 12:1.

2 1 Sam. 16; 2 Sam. 5.

3 Deut. 31:6; Heb. 13:5.

4 Rom. 12:12.

5 Gal. 6:9.

6 Eph. 4:2; Prov. 15:18; Col. 3:12.

7 Rom. 2:7.

8 Exod. 34:6; Num. 14:18; Neh. 9:17 are just some examples.

[9]   1 Cor. 13:4.

[10] Gal. 5:22. The Greek word for fruit is singular, with each of the qualities listed forming part of the whole. The NIV uses the word 'forbearance'.

[11] Ps. 37:7.

Chapter 13: The Samaritan Woman

[1]   Such as where Jesus touches the leper, in defiance of Jewish purity laws, Matt. 8:3.

[2]   See Acts 8:4–8; Acts 10.

[3]   See Neh. 4:1–2.

[4]   Luke 10:25–37.

[5]   See Deut. 11:26–32.

[6]   Matt. 28:18–20.

[7]   Mark 16:15.

[8]   Acts 1:8.

[9]   See Exod. 20:16; Deut. 19:15–21.

[10] Isa. 43:12.

[11] Ps. 107:2.

[12] 1 John 1:1.

[13] 1 John 1:3.

[14] Matt. 5:13–16.

[15] 2 Cor. 5:20.

[16] 1 Cor. 2:1–5.

[17] See for example David Watson, *Discipleship* (London: Hodder & Stoughton, 2014).

[18] Matt. 23:1–36.

[19] Luke 7:36.

[20] See for example Matt. 9:10–13; Luke 19:1–10.

[21] John 13:35.

Chapter 14: The Widow

[1] See for example Lev. 27:30–33; Num. 18.
[2] See Mal. 3:8–18.
[3] Prov. 22:9.
[4] Matt. 23:23.
[5] Acts 11:29; 1 Cor. 16:1–4.
[6] 2 Cor. 9:5–8.
[7] Luke 6:38.
[8] https://www.theguardian.com/science/2015/jan/26/rationing-ravens-merciful-monkeys-can-animals-be-altruistic (accessed 14 June 2022).
[9] See for example https://www.nationalgeographic.com/animals/article/140221-elephants-poaching-empathy-grief-extinction-science (accessed 6 December 2022).
[10] Matt. 10:8.
[11] 1 John 3:1.
[12] Luke 19:8.
[13] Lev. 5:16; Num. 5:7.
[14] https://www.science.org/doi/10.1126/science.1150952 cited in https://www.psychologytoday.com/us/blog/master-your-success/202001/the-real-challenge-generosity (accessed 13 June 2022).
[15] https://www.medicalnewstoday.com/articles/318406#The-neural-underpinnings (accessed 6 December 2022); see also https://www.nature.com/articles/ncomms15964.pdf (accessed 15 June 2022).

Chapter 15: Judas

[1] Jewish day of the week: Sunday.
[2] See Michael Green, *The Message of Matthew* (Leicester: Inter-Varsity Press, 1988), p. 268.
[3] Exod. 21:32.
[4] John 5:7; Acts 17:8–15.

5   See Bruce Milne, *The Message of John* (Leicester: Inter-Varsity Press, 1993), p. 202.

6   Luke 22:48.

7   Matt. 26:50.

8   The origin of this appears to be the legend of the Judas tree – where Judas hanged in hell and Jesus came and cut him down, and a tradition in the Orthodox church. See https://archbishop-cranmer.com/holy-saturday-the-harrowing-of-hell/ (accessed 6 December 2022). The idea is often quoted including in https://dwightlongenecker.com/judas-jesus-go/ (accessed 6 December 2022).

9   For a moving account of trusting God in our circumstances, see John Goldingay, *Walk On: Life, Loss, Trust, and Other Realities* (Ada, MI: Baker Academic, 2002), pp. 162–173 and Ps. 41:9.

10 https://synapse.ucsf.edu/articles/2017/12/05/psychology-be-trayal (accessed 19 July 2022).

11 Act 3, Scene 1.

12 For a more detailed description of the ethical framework for counsellors see https://www.bacp.co.uk/events-and-resources/ethics-and-standards/ethical-framework-for-the-counselling-professions/ (accessed 6 December 2022).

13 There is a great deal of literature available on the stages of grieving. For a simple explanation of one of several ways of looking at grief see https://www.cruse.org.uk/understanding-grief/effects-of-grief/five-stages-of-grief/ (accessed 6 December 2022).

14 https://www.psychologytoday.com/us/blog/anger-in-the-age-entitlement/201401/trust-and-betrayal (accessed 19 July 2022).

15 Rom. 12:17.

16 See for example Matt. 6:14–15.

Chapter 16: Herod Antipas

1   Matt. 2:1–20.

2   Matt. 2:22.

3 In Matt. 14:1–6; Mark 6:14–22; Luke 3:1,19–20; 8:3; 9:7–9; 13:31–33; 23:7–15; Acts 4:27; 13:1.

4 See https://jewishencyclopedia.com/articles/7598-herod-i (accessed 6 December 2022).

5 See https://www.jewishencyclopedia.com/articles/1597-antipas-herod-antipas (accessed 6 December 2022).

6 She was the daughter of Aristobulus IV, Herod Antipas' murdered brother, and his wife, Berenice.

7 See Pauline Rose Clance, *The Imposter Phenomenon: Overcoming the Fear That Haunts Your Success* (Atlanta, GA: Peachtree Publications, 1985).

8 See https://www.berkeleywellbeing.com/imposter-syndrome.html (accessed 29 June 2022) for further details.

9 See https://www.psychologytoday.com/us/basics/perfectionism (accessed 2 July 2022).

10 See https://www.nhs.uk/mental-health/conditions/anxiety/ (accessed 6 December 2022).

11 There may have been other aspects such as an understandable reluctance to return to Egypt.

12 Exod. 4:10.

13 Judg. 6:15.

14 Ps. 34:10.

15 Matt. 6:28–30.

16 Zeph. 3:17.

17 1 John 3:1.

18 For example Rom. 8:15.

19 Rom. 8:17.

20 John 11:25–26.

21 Rom. 8:31–32,37–39.

Chapter 17: Pilate

1 https://www.youtube.com/watch?v=5mYDyxMDwaw (accessed 6 December 2022).

2 Question Time, 7 July 2022.

3   See the previous chapter on Herod Antipas.

4   See William Barclay, *The Gospel of Matthew Vol. 2* (Edinburgh: The Saint Andrew Press, 1957), pp. 394–398.

5   See for example Exod. 20:4.

6   Matt. 27:14.

7   John 19:12.

8   Tom Wright, *John for Everyone: Part 2, Chapters 11–21* (London: SPCK, 2002), p. 122.

9   See Milne, *The Message of John*, p. 272.

10 John 19:15.

11 See for example https://english.stackexchange.com/questions/177947/where-did-the-phrase-washing-ones-hands-of-originate (accessed 6 December 2022).

12 There is also a curious echo of the Jewish practice of washing hands in the case of unsolved murders: see Deut. 21:1–9.

13 See for example https://www.learnreligions.com/jewish-hand-washing-rituals-2076317 (accessed 13 July 2022).

14 https://hermeneutics.stackexchange.com/questions/21586/was-washing-ones-hands-to-show-innocence-as-pilate-did-a-common-ritual-in-the (accessed 6 December 2022).

15 Luke 23:25.

16 This topic is too large to be considered here, but such teaching is clearly erroneous.

17 https://www.psychologytoday.com/us/blog/the-craving-brain/201905/surrender (accessed 6 December 2022).

18 https://www.aa.org/the-twelve-steps (accessed 6 December 2022).

19 Written by Judson W. Van DeVenter (1855–1939) in 1896.

20 See for example Josh. 6, in particular v. 21, and 1 Sam. 31, just two of many examples.

21 Perhaps the most well-known passage on this theme is Eph. 6:10–18.

22 Jas 4:7.

23 Matt. 16:23.

24 Luke 4:13.

25 Luke 22:39–46.

26 Mark 15:32.

27 John 19:30; Luke 23:46.

28 Ps. 9:10.

[29] John 15:2.

[30] https://poets.org/poem/do-not-go-gentle-good-night (accessed 6 December 2022).

Chapter 18: Thomas

[1] Jewish days of the week: Friday and Saturday.

[2] Jewish day of the week: Sunday.

[3] John 21:2.

[4] See https://www.thoughtco.com/little-matchstick-girl-short-story-739298 (accessed 6 December 2022).

[5] There are some notable exceptions such as 'Weep With Me' (Rend Collective), 'We Have Sung Our Songs of Victory (How Long?)' (Stuart Townend), 'Blessed Be Your Name' (Matt Redman) and 'Praise You In This Storm' (Casting Crowns).

[6] John 20:29.

[7] R. Roberts in David J. Atkinson and David H. Field, *New Dictionary of Christian Ethics and Pastoral Theology* (Leicester: Inter-Varsity Press, 1995), p. 454, lists forthrightness, promise-keeping, intellectual honesty, sincerity, and self-transparency.

[8] Christian B. Miller in https://psyche.co/ideas/more-than-just-truth-telling-honesty-is-a-virtue-to-cultivate (accessed 26 July 2022).

[9] See https://www.theguardian.com/science/2006/jun/28/psychology.uknews (accessed 25 July 2022).

[10] Exod. 20:14–16.

[11] Eph. 4:25.

[12] Eph. 4:15.

[13] Christian Miller, in the article cited above, points out that other motives for honesty include justice, friendship and duty.

[14] See http://emotionalprocessing.org/somatization/ (accessed 25 July 2022).

[15] See for example https://www.news-medical.net/health/How-does-Stress-Affect-Your-Immune-System.aspx (accessed 6 December 2022).

16 See https://www.pastoralsupervision.org.uk/ (accessed 6 December 2022) for further details including a list of pastoral supervisors.
17 Matt. 26:40.

Chapter 19: Stephen

1 Messiah.
2 https://hebrewwordlessons.com/2020/01/26/hineni-here-i-am/ (accessed 30 July 2022).
3 For a moving story about one journey of forgiveness, see *Finding Our Voice*, 2019, pp. 59–62.
4 Lewis B. Smedes, *Forgive and Forget: Healing the Hurts We Don't Deserve* (New York: HarperCollins, 1996), p. 38.
5 See Claire and Steve Musters, *Grace-Filled Marriage: Strengthened and Transformed Through God's Redemptive Love* (Milton Keynes: Authentic Media, 2021) for a moving account of this in a marriage situation.
6 Dr Fred Luskin is a professor at the Institute for Transpersonal Psychology and director of the Stanford University Forgiveness Projects.
7 See Frederic Luskin, *Forgive for Good: A Proven Prescription for Health and Happiness* (New York: HarperCollins, 2003).
8 See https://positivepsychology.com/psychology-of-forgiveness/ (accessed 30 July 2022).
9 Shauna L. Shapiro, *Rewire Your Mind: Discover the Science and Practice of Mindfulness* (London: Aster, 2020).
10 Jeannie Kendall, *Held in Your Bottle* (Milton Keynes: Authentic Media, 2021).
11 See for example https://www.psychologytoday.com/us/blog/stronger-the-broken-places/201712/reframing (accessed 6 December 2022).
12 The story of David and Bathsheba in 2 Sam. 11 and 12 is a biblical example of this.
13 Matt. 22:39.
14 See https://www.rd.com/list/inspiring-forgiveness-stories/ and https://www.theforgivenessproject.com/stories-of-forgiveness/ for some examples (both accessed 30 July 2022).

[15] R.T. Kendall, *Total Forgiveness: Achieving God's Greatest Challenge* (London: Hodder & Stoughton, 2010), p. 6.

[16] See https://positivepsychology.com/forgiveness-benefits/ (accessed 30 July 2022) for a summary of some of the research on this and other aspects of forgiveness, also Everett L. Worthington, *Forgiveness and Reconciliation: Theory and Application* (New York: Routledge, 2006).

[17] Ps. 103:9–12.

[18] See for example Lev. 4.

[19] Jer. 31:34.

[20] 1 John 1:9.

[21] Rom. 3:23.

[22] 1 John 1:8–10, MSG.

[23] Luke 11:4.

[24] Matt. 6:14–15.

[25] Matt. 18:21.

[26] 1 Cor. 13:5.

[27] Matt. 18:21–35.

[28] Matt. 18:35.

[29] Mark 11:25; Matt. 5:23–24.

[30] Luke 23:34.

[31] See for example 1 Cor. 1:10; 2 Cor. 13:11.

[32] Col. 3:13.

[33] Tom Wright, *Matthew for Everyone: Part 2, Chapters 16–28* (London: SPCK, 2002), pp. 39–40.

[34] See for example John and Carol Arnott, *Grace and Forgiveness* (Toronto: Catch the Fire, 2015).

[35] Smedes, *Forgive and Forget: Healing the Hurts We Don't Deserve*, p. 152.

[36] Luke 23:34.

Chapter 20: Paul

[1] This is an estimate, the exact proportion depends of course on the view we take on the authorship of Hebrews.

2   Acts 9:1–19.

3   Phil. 3:5–6.

4   Gal. 1:17–18.

5   Acts 11:25.

6   We see this in the fact that in Acts 14:12 he was assumed to be Zeus by the people in Lystra.

7   John Mark had earlier left their journey prematurely (Acts 13:13); we do not know why. Later Barnabas wanted to bring John Mark back to join them, but Paul refused (Acts 15:36–39).

8   In 2 Cor. 12:14 he speaks of coming for a third time, so clearly there had been a visit in between the long stay and writing 2 Corinthians. Some scholars think that 2 Cor. 10 – 12 was originally a separate letter, perhaps even the letter mentioned in 2 Cor. 7:8 which Paul is aware may have caused them distress.

9   2 Cor. 12:14.

10 2 Cor. 2:1–4.

11 See for example 1 Cor. 1:1; 2:1–7.

12 Acts 19:23–40, note verse 30.

13 Richard Dormandy, *The Madness of St Paul: How St Paul Discovered the Love of God* (Chawton: Redemptorist Publications, 2011), p. 50.

14 2 Cor. 12:7.

15 2 Cor. 12:9.

16 2 Cor. 2:14.

17 2 Cor. 4:3.

18 2 Cor. 4:7.

19 2 Cor. 5:1–4.

20 See Thomas Dixon, *Weeping Britannia: Portrait of a Nation in Tears* (Oxford: Oxford University Press, 2016).

21 https://www.youtube.com/watch?v=iCvmsMzlF7o&t=46s (accessed 2 August 2022). This talk has been watched by more than 18 million people.

22 Places like this have been pioneered by the work of Renew Wellbeing. See https://www.renewwellbeing.org.uk/ (accessed 6 August 2022).

Finding Our Voice

*Unsung lives from the Bible
resonating with stories from today*

Jeannie Kendall

In *Finding Our Voice*, powerful modern-day testimony intermingles with the often raw experiences of those we read about in the pages of the Bible – unnamed characters who have, in a sense, never had a 'voice' of their own.

Jeannie Kendall brings these unnamed people to life, reimagining their story from the biblical text in order to hear their voice today.

The issues and experiences unpacked in these reflections are then mirrored by a relevant testimony from someone who has dealt with similar situations in today's world, and then pastoral insight given on the topics raised.

978-1-78893-037-6

Held in Your Bottle

*Exploring the value of tears in the Bible
and in our lives today*

Jeannie Kendall

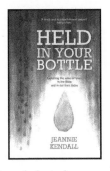

Combining contemporary stories, biblical narrative and psychological insights, *Held in Your Bottle* looks at the many reasons why we cry, and why these tears are important to our wellbeing and to God.

Each of these emotions is explored by a modern-day story mirroring a retelling of a relevant Bible character's experience. Insightful reflections then help us understand the issues raised.

978-1-78893-171-7

Authentic

We trust you enjoyed reading this book from Authentic. If you want to be informed of any new titles from this author and other releases you can sign up to the Authentic newsletter by scanning below:

Online:
authenticmedia.co.uk

Follow us: